# MESSIAH

# MESSIAH

*The Gospel according to
Handel's Oratorio*

Roger A. Bullard

WILLIAM B. EERDMANS PUBLISHING COMPANY
GRAND RAPIDS, MICHIGAN

Copyright © 1993 by Wm. B. Eerdmans Publishing Co.
255 Jefferson Ave. S.E., Grand Rapids, Mich. 49503

Printed in the United States of America

00 99 98 97 96 95     7 6 5 4 3 2


**Library of Congress Cataloging-in-Publication Data**

Bullard, Roger Aubrey.
Messiah: the Gospel according to Handel's oratorio /
Roger Bullard.
p.        cm.
ISBN 0-8028-0125-0
1. Handel, George Frideric, 1685-1759. Messiah.
2. Bible — Criticism, interpretation, etc.   I. Title.
ML410.H13B88     1993
782.23 — dc20                          93-24710
                                          CIP
                                          MN

# Contents

*For
Carol
and
Kenneth
and
Floyd*

# Introduction

I HAD FORGOTTEN the incident until sitting down to write this introduction. In a dormitory bull session one evening during my college years, I argued with a fellow student that the words to Handel's *Messiah* made no sense, that the text was disjointed, random, and incoherent. He said I was wrong. I was. At the time I did not know enough about the Bible, literary structure, or musical form to perceive what is in fact a skillfully crafted, well-rounded statement of Christian doctrine.

This book is written for the benefit of those who sing and hear *Messiah* with perhaps as little background for an appreciation of the words as I had at that time.

The text of the oratorio was compiled by Charles Jennens, a friend of Handel who also wrote libretti (texts) for others of the composer's large vocal works. The words come entirely from the Bible, both Old and New Testaments, though quite often liberties are taken with the text. The King James Version is the basis for all the passages used except those from the Psalms, where an older version found in the Book of Common Prayer was followed.

This book will proceed by examining each of the fifty-three sections of *Messiah* in more than one context. First, the passage of Scripture will be looked at in its original literary setting. This involves more than simply explaining the meaning of a few sentences in the context of the paragraph in which they are found in the Bible.

More broadly, it will often involve seeing the ideas against the religious, social, and political background of the biblical writer's own time. The first task, then, is to examine what the writer meant by his words and what they meant to his first audience.

Some of the Old Testament passages selected by Jennens are quoted in the New Testament as well. Here is another context to examine. Great literature speaks not only to the constants in human nature, but to the flux of our experience as well. What is well said at one time and place may be read at another time and place with an overlay of meaning not originally intended by the author himself or herself. Christians have from the very beginning read the Jewish Scripture in the light of their experience with Jesus Christ. We must see how the New Testament writers found meaning in Hebrew Scripture, and what interpretive continuum links the original context and the Christian appropriation of it, whether in the New Testament or in later literature.

Having viewed a passage in its original biblical setting, and in more than one biblical setting where that applies, we must then look at the context within the literary structure of the oratorio. In doing that, we will discover how what could easily have been a random pastiche of Bible quotations has become an artfully articulated expression of Christian thought.

Jennens of course did not have the methods of modern biblical study at his disposal, and would be surprised at some of the things found here in his text — although we ourselves might be surprised to discover how much of this would have been familiar to him. Jennens clearly knew the Bible and Christian theology. In this libretto he has taken a relatively few biblical passages and used them to state theology, sometimes by placing those passages in considerable tension with their contexts. Yet what he created has its own right to exist as a work of art. I invite the reader to share with me the exploration of these passages as they fit within the biblical setting as well as within the context of Handel's massive work.

At the beginning of each section or sequence of sections in our guide, the text of the oratorio is provided, along with the appropriate Scripture reference.

Within the body of the commentary that follows, save for quotations of the libretto, most Scripture references are quoted from the New Revised Standard Version of 1990. This translation stands in the direct line of the King James tradition, and consequently its phraseology will be as close to that of the oratorio text as contemporary English usage and current biblical scholarship will allow. On a few occasions another version has been cited, such as the Revised English Bible of 1989 (REB); these places are duly noted.

At one point I have referred to the preface to the King James Version. This remarkable document, "The Translators to the Reader," is no longer published along with the Bible. The only place it is readily accessible today is in Geddes MacGregor's *A Literary History of the Bible* (Nashville: Abingdon Press, 1968), pp. 220-42. It is worth reading. Almost certainly the reception accorded the various translations of the twentieth century would have been quite different had this preface been familiar to the hostile critics of our recent versions.

I refer on numerous occasions to what I call an "ancient Greek translation" of the Old Testament. This version is known as the Septuagint. It was produced by Jewish scholars in Alexandria, Egypt, in the third and second centuries before Christ. It was intended for the use of the Greek-speaking Jews of the Diaspora, but when the Christian movement began, with its literature produced in Greek, the Septuagint quickly became the Christian Bible, or that portion that would later be known as the Old Testament. This ancient translation is crucially important in the endeavor to reconstruct the original text of the Hebrew Scriptures in places where the text is in doubt. At a number of points in *Messiah*, passages are used which are textually uncertain in the original language. These are usually those in which the reader will find the greatest differences between the oratorio text and various recent translations. It is generally in connection with these passages that I have referred to this "ancient translation."

Several times also I have referred to the Latin Bible. This is the version known as the Vulgate, the work of the great St. Jerome, patron saint of translators, who died A.D. 420. His translation was to become the standard Bible used by the Catholic Church — that is, Western Christianity — throughout the Middle Ages and well into modern times. The translators of the King James Version were well acquainted with it, and their translation, though made from the original languages of Hebrew and Greek, often betrays its influence.

Christians who hold to a very conservative view of biblical inspiration will find a few matters in the commentary with which they disagree. This will particularly pertain to the idea that the book of the great prophet Isaiah consists of two portions, most of the first of which (chapters 1–39) is associated with the eighth-century prophet Isaiah of Jerusalem, and the second of which (chapters 40–66) is attributed to one or more anonymous prophets of the exilic and postexilic periods of biblical history. Scholars know these latter chapters as Deutero-Isaiah or Second Isaiah. Some speak of a Trito- or Third Isaiah as well. In the attempt to avoid scholarly jargon, I have referred to the author(s) of these chapters simply as the exilic Isaiah, or the later Isaiah. For the most part, however, the interpretations of biblical text found in this commentary are the consensus of scholars of all persuasions.

Christians of more liberal persuasion may be offended by interpretations of some passages which may appear to be too overtly messianic. Jewish readers may quite often find themselves in a strange, unfamiliar world at this point. I must ask these friends to remember that the commentary is not on the text of the Bible as such, but on the text of Handel's oratorio *Messiah*. In understanding this oratorio, we must work with its own presuppositions, which are those of the Church of England of the eighteenth century, and, indeed, of the Christian church throughout most of history.

At the end of each section or sequence I have added a few modest reflections on the music of the oratorio. The author, it should be emphasized, is neither a musician nor the son of a musician, and his comments do not presume to edify the professional. They are simply the ideas of an appreciative music lover hoping to guide other lay listeners to a better understanding of what they hear.

*Messiah* is a magisterial piece of music, and there is always something new about each singing of it, for both performers and listeners alike. It is also a magnificent theological statement in artistic form, and it is particularly toward the appreciation of this aspect that this book is dedicated.

Biblical scholars who favor me by reading these pages will recognize the debts I owe to those who have thought along these lines before me. Other readers will not be particularly interested, and I have not burdened them. Other debts of a more personal nature should be acknowledged: my wife Carol for the encouragement in developing the idea; my friend and colleague Gene Purcell for a careful and critical reading of a very rough draft; Lynn Medlin for transforming that draft into readable copy; and to my editor Jon Pott for the sensitivity and practical wisdom with which he transformed that copy into a real book.

# PART I

# 1. Overture

A thousand years or so before the birth of Jesus the Messiah, there was another messiah. He was not the first — there was one before him — and there would be others after him. But he is the one who counts. His name was David, and he was king of Israel.

He was a handsome figure, shrewd in his dealings and valiant in doing battle. He evoked admiration in women and fierce loyalty in men. David was not perfect; there was a squalid side to his character, an unsavory dimension to his rule. Some in Israel would never forget that, but others in the coming generations would think of him only as the ideal king, the Anointed One against whom all later ones would be compared and tested. He stood at the head of the lineage of Israel's kings.

In those ancient days, kings were not crowned when they assumed office. Rather, a priest would take a ram's horn filled with olive oil and pour it over the head of the one who had been chosen to lead. This was anointing, and the king was thus the Anointed One — as he is often called in the Old Testament. In Hebrew, the Anointed One is *meshiach,* which comes over into English as "Messiah." The Greek equivalent to this is *christos,* or Christ.

The first of these anointed kings was actually Saul. But beginning a new dynasty, David followed him. Then came David's son and successor Solomon. On Solomon's death, the kingdom split in two, as the northern tribes revolted against the house of David and set up their own kingdom in the north. Somewhat confusingly, this is known as Israel. In the south the line of David ruled over the kingdom of Judah, with its capital in David's city, Jerusalem.

In the Old Testament the word *meshiach* is used only of Saul, David, Solomon, and the kings of Judah, except for one place in which Cyrus of Persia is referred to figuratively as God's anointed. The Israelite kingship is thus the matrix out of which was to grow the hope of Israel for its true messiah.

Jesus is, of course, the messiah whom Handel's oratorio concerns. Yet in the whole performance of the music we will never hear his name and we will never hear his voice. The text will tell us of the *promise* of Messiah, the *coming* of Messiah, the *ministry* of Messiah, the *suffering, death,* and *resurrection* of Messiah, and of his *exaltation* and *eternal reign.* But it will all be told by indirection. We will not hear his teaching in the Sermon on the Mount, we will not hear the seven last words from the cross, and we will not be told the story of the empty tomb. Scripture will be used to tell the story in ways that point beyond the immediate meaning of the texts chosen.

But the hope begins with David, anointed by the venerable old prophet Samuel to be king in place of Saul. Victorious in his battles as king, David wished to build a temple for God. But through the prophet Nathan, God told David that he was not to build God a house. Rather, God would build David a house — a dynasty of kings — that would rule from Zion forever.

Mighty David! Long after his death, as the line of his descendants held sway over Judah, he was remembered as the ideal king, and the patriotic protocols of the kingdom called for whatever king sat on the throne to be honored as would be David himself. Some of the Psalms — Psalms 2, 20, 21, 45, 72, 110 — sing the praises of the king, God's Anointed One. Psalm 72 sounds very much like a prayer at the inauguration of an American president, calling on God for the success, wisdom, and justice of the king, that the Anointed One might rule over a nation at peace, over a prosperous people. At times the prophets also would speak of the king in terms reminiscent of David.

But beginning in the eighth century before Christ, when we first begin to pick up their words, the message of the prophets is somber, laden with a burden of impending doom. These seers — Amos, Hosea, Isaiah, Micah, the young Jeremiah — were not peering across centuries to see what would come about long after their own time. Their inspired prophetic insight consisted in the gift of perceiving divine action in their own time. When they predicted the future, as sometimes they did, it was a relatively near future. There was a kind of prophetic syllogism. They made an observation about their historical circumstances: God's people are sinful. Then they interpreted that observation in the light of what they believed

4

about the nature of God: God punishes sin. From this they drew a conclusion: God will punish his people. Whether the agent of that punishment would be Egypt or Assyria or Babylonia ultimately did not matter. God would act in history and use historical forces to bring on his own people just punishment for their sin.

Meanwhile the kingship suffered decline. The kings who followed after David were not always just or wise or victorious or handsome. They could be vicious and unjust and foolish and cowardly. But on occasions of state they would still be addressed as the Anointed of God. When the royal retinue passed by in stately procession, the people might feel keenly the contrast between the traditional language of royal praise and the actual character and accomplishments of their own king. Somewhere in this tension between the ideal and the actual was born the hope that in God's good time a worthy successor to David would come again to the throne of Judah.

But then came instead that time of judgment predicted by the prophets, the Day of the Lord, as Amos and others had called it. The enemy arrived and vanquished God's people. For the kingdom of Israel in the north the year was 721, as Assyria invaded and captured the land, scattering its population to the winds of history. For Judah the end came in 587. The Babylonians captured Jerusalem, destroyed the Temple that had been built by Solomon, and took the cream of the population into exile in Babylonia.

There these exiles lived bereft of king and temple and bereft, as it seemed, of all God's promises. The promises to Abraham seemed canceled; they were far away from their home, the land promised to their ancestor Abraham, the Promised Land of old. The promises to David appeared to be annulled: there was no king in Zion. But to sustain the people, the hope of a coming Anointed One worthy of David leaped above the plane of history to become an expectation of the future. God would restore the kingdom; an Anointed of God would once again rule God's people. The Messiah was becoming an eschatological figure; the messianic hope was growing in profundity.

There in exile the prophets began to speak a new message. The same prophetic gift was at work, but the syllogism changed. The prophets looked at their circumstances and made an observation: God's people are suffering. They analyzed this in the light of what they believed about God's nature: God is faithful to his people. From this they drew a conclusion: God will redeem his people. God will bring them back to their land.

This prediction, like the predictions of the preexilic prophets, was fulfilled. Eventually there was a return to the homeland, though never a restoration of the Davidic kingdom. Yet the words of the prophets, of those who spoke doom and those who spoke benison, were remembered and treasured long after the immediate fulfillments had passed into history. For the Jews believed that those words conveyed something terrible and splendid about God. Wherever there was rebellion against God, the words of the preexilic prophets would reverberate. Wherever people were oppressed, in whatever circumstance, the oracles of the exilic prophets would resonate to a new frequency.

And so, after the coming of Jesus, it was with the Christians who began to use the prophets. Where people felt themselves oppressed under a burden of sin, the words of hope and redemption spoke anew, and they saw in Jesus — the Anointed One, the Messiah — a grander fulfillment of prophetic promise than the prophets themselves had dreamed of. They found the ancient oracles pregnant with meaning unfathomed in the prophets' own times. And they saw in Jesus the fulfillment of the old hope of a coming King, a coming Son of David, who restored no earthly throne, but of whose kingdom there would be no end, and who would reign forever and ever.

~

THE SOMBER opening chords of the overture place us in the darkness of the exile, away from our roots, bereft of our identity, with no hope for present or future. But the somber chords introduce no funeral dirge, no march of the dead. Gloom there is, but there is stateliness in the gloom, something of a refusal to believe that death is all that awaits. The musical line moves higher through the dark, moved by the faith that God has not forsaken his people, that a future yet lies ahead. As the brilliant fugue opens, the hope shines through, lively with faith; the music works its way into a crescendo before the movement resolves itself on chords once more somber. But these closing chords are now informed by a sustaining confidence. It is not despair sounding forth here, but firmness of spirit. Something has been moving in these depths that will issue in a new beginning. Herein is the hope: God will yet act.

## 2. TENOR RECITATIVE

Comfort ye, comfort ye my people, saith your God. Speak ye comfortably to Jerusalem, and cry unto her, that her warfare is accomplish'd, that her iniquity is pardon'd.

The voice of him that crieth in the wilderness: Prepare ye the way of the Lord, make straight in the desert a highway for our God.

## 3. TENOR ARIA

Ev'ry valley shall be exalted, and ev'ry mountain and hill made low, the crooked straight, and the rough places plain.

## 4. CHORUS

And the glory of the Lord shall be revealed. And all flesh shall see it together, for the mouth of the Lord hath spoken it. *(Isaiah 40:1-5, modified)*

Cutting through the gloom of exile come words of assurance, the opening lines of the second part of the book of the prophet Isaiah.

7

This book, as we noted, is divided into two parts. The first is associated with the eighth-century prophet Isaiah of Jerusalem; the second, beginning with chapter 40, is thought by most scholars to be a collection of prophecies from anonymous prophets of the exilic and postexilic periods. Many think chapters 40–55 are the literary remains of a nameless prophet of the exile known as the Second Isaiah.

These words are spoken to the Jewish community in Babylonian exile, who in their land of alien sojourning, by whose waters they sang in Psalm 137 of hanging their harps on the willows, hear the prophet announcing a word of comfort from none other than their ancestral God.

This is the God who, two hundred years earlier, had commanded the prophet Hosea to speak to Israel the disowning words: "You are not my people and I am not your God" (Hosea 1:9). But now there is a reversal. The welcome word of comfort is stated and repeated, as God reclaims them as "my people." This is said in the name of "your God." The alienation is ended. Separation from the land represented separation from God, but God now reclaims his people and will return them to their heritage.

The prophet Micah had asked, "What is the sin of Judah? Is it not Jerusalem?" (Micah 1:5 Revised English Bible). David's capital city had become crystallized as a symbol of the people's sin, but now Jerusalem is to be told that her time of alienation is over. Her warfare is accomplished — "her term of service" is a better translation. Her sentence has been served. Her iniquity has been finally dealt with in a way open to God alone; it has been pardoned. Sin can be punished, but it cannot be dealt with in an ultimate way until it has been forgiven.

These are the prophet's words of assurance to God's exiled people, to the desolate city of whom the poet spoke:

How lonely sits the city
    that once was full of people!

(Lamentations 1:1)

The God who had brought them up from the land of Egypt would now lead them home. "Speak comfortably" of course means "speak comfortingly."

The prophet's next words are not well construed in the King James Version, which the libretto is faithfully following here. Any modern translation will capture the real structure:

> A voice cries out:
> "In the wilderness prepare the way of the LORD,
> make straight in the desert a highway for our God."

What the voice cries are two perfectly parallel lines: wilderness/desert; prepare/make straight; the way/a highway; the LORD/our God. This parallel structuring was crucially important in Hebrew poetry, and this prophet, like most of the Hebrew prophets, was a poet.

The image here is of a highway being built straight across the desert from Babylonia, the land of exile, to Israel, the once more Promised Land. Ordinarily the traveler going from Babylonia to Israel would follow the curvature of the Fertile Crescent, avoiding the desert; but this road is to cut directly through the arid wilderness. It is the Lord who will be traveling that road, leading his people homeward. While serving their sentence in exile, the people may have been bereft of king, land, and temple, but even while God executed his punishment, he had not abandoned them, and he was now to lead them to restoration.

The form these words assume in the text of the oratorio has another significance beyond that of the exilic prophet. An ancient translation of these words into Greek had indeed rendered, "The voice of one crying in the wilderness." It is this version of the oracle that the evangelists Matthew, Mark, and Luke quote and which John refers to when they introduce the figure of John the Baptist, a latter-day prophet who, like Elijah long before him, was a rough-clad figure of the wilderness. Jewish tradition, based on the closing words of Malachi (which is not the last book of the canon of Jewish Scripture as it is of the Christian Old Testament), held that Elijah,

9

who had been taken directly up into heaven, would return as a herald of God's Anointed One, the Messiah. Christian tradition saw John the Baptist as precisely this figure, emerging from the wilderness to announce the coming of the Lord — the advent of Jesus.

Just as all four of the gospel writers begin the story of Jesus' ministry with the witness borne to him by John, the oratorio begins with this harking forward to John's announcement by reinterpreting the words of the ancient exilic prophet.

But this reinterpretation is not a misinterpretation. The Baptist's call to repentance in preparation for Messiah's coming is quite in line with the prophet's announcement of pardon, his proclamation that God would lead his forgiven people along a broad highway home. The traditions transmitted by the people of Israel from their past were constantly being shaped and reinterpreted; the evangelists' connection of this passage with the proclamation of John the Baptist is simply taking this ancient process a step further.

The tenor is quoting the words of the prophet in exile, but as we listen we hear them merge into the words of John the Baptist, announcing the coming of God's Anointed.

The tenor aria continues the poetic imagery of the highway. It is a picture familiar to all who have seen modern highways under construction. Cuts are made through high terrain and the earth removed is used to build up low spots, to make the grades less steep. Ways are found by the engineers to reduce the curves to manageable proportions. This is the imagery of our prophet/poet: "Every valley shall be exalted, and every mountain and hill made low."

But this poetry, like all fine poetry, is open to meaning beyond its literal semantic value. We must read this in the light of the Virgin Mary's theme as she sings in the Magnificat:

> He has brought down the powerful from their thrones,
>     and lifted up the lowly.
>
> (Luke 1:52)

Messiah's coming will bring justice, vindication for the downtrodden at the expense of those who have fostered injustice. The preexilic words of Amos, who so insisted on social justice, who condemned those "who trample the head of the poor into the dust of the earth" (Amos 2:7), are not obviated by Messiah's advent. The old words of judgment maintain validity and force.

"The LORD of hosts has a day against all that is proud and lofty," wrote Isaiah of Jerusalem, "against all that is lifted up and high" (Isaiah 2:12). There will be no obstacle to the Lord in his coming, whether mountains in the desert or mountains of human presumption and arrogance. The highway will be made straight, level, even. The prophet sees God as determined in his intention to vindicate his people as he was determined that they should pay for their sin. The crooked will be made straight, and the rough places made into a wide and open plain — and the glory of the Lord will be revealed in this act.

The glory of the Lord is a theme in the Old Testament. The literal term used in Hebrew is "the weight of the Lord," his heaviness, as it were, his overwhelming importance. (The Greek translators realized that this would make no sense in Greek, so they used a term meaning "fame, reputation." Jerome, in putting it into Latin, chose the word *gloria,* which has given us our term.) The glory of the Lord was revealed in powerful deeds, when God made a manifest statement; it might be pictured as accompanied by fire or cloud. The term is taken over in the New Testament, where it is associated with Christ. The Letter to the Hebrews opens: "Long ago God spoke to our ancestors in many and various ways by the prophets, but in these last days he has spoken to us by a Son. . . . He is the reflection of God's glory . . ." (Hebrews 1:1-3). The glory of the Lord is a theme returned to often in the text of Handel's oratorio, and we must be alert to its occurrence.

So the glory of God, the statement made by God in the powerful act of redeeming his people from oppression, becomes in larger context the Messiah himself, who will redeem God's people from a bondage to sin more profound than the subjugation by Babylonian exile. This is what will be revealed: God's redeeming activity; and all humanity shall see it together. The return across the desert highway will be of the Jews going home, but that act of glory, that revelation of God's purposes, will be a witness to the nations, to all the worlds, of a salvation available to all through the God of Israel, who called Israel as a light to the nations.

When Matthew and Mark quote the prophet in referring to John the Baptist, they close the quotation with "make his ways straight." But Luke sees more in the prophet's words. He continues the quotation until he comes to this point, which he cites from the ancient Greek translation: "and all flesh shall see the salvation of God" (Luke 3:6).

Here are words of assurance for all God's people, Jew and Gentile alike, pictured in God's promise of redemption and restoration. Here are words guaranteed by the authority of the source of the prophet's message, "for the mouth of the Lord has spoken." In section 9, "O Thou That Tellest Good Tidings," we will be returning to this passage from Isaiah 40.

~

SILENCE follows the closing chord of the overture. The music begins again, softly. It broods and ripples, like the primeval waters of chaos over which the Spirit of God hovers at the beginning of creation, just before God spoke light into existence. The darkness of exile is profound, but there is hope alive within it. The obscurity is pierced by the tenor's first note, like the first ray of light illuminating the primordial dark. His rising line is the breaking dawn of a new day for God's people, falling back into serene assurance: "Comfort ye my people."

"Saith your God" is sung in three forceful notes, rising with the hope rising in human hearts, and then repeated, soaring to a height of resurrected confidence. The singer lingers over the words "that her warfare," building a tension for the coming announcement, as the phrase "is accomplished" comes down in a sudden cascade, and is not repeated. It is final. The same resoluteness comes on "that her iniquity is pardoned," but this time, lest the news be too good to be believed, the phrase is repeated, with a drawn out flourish.

The command of the Baptist is strong and straightforward and brooking of no escape. The time has come. There are no repeats here. In no uncertain words — or notes — we are told of the highway that is "for our God," with that phrase uttered with descending finality, like the "saith your God" in its ascending sureness in the first phrases.

The aria is an exultation in joy, with every phrase shaped to its purpose. We thrill with the exaltation of the valleys, we hold our breath at the lowering of the mountains and hills. We hear the crooked being made straight. The tenor requires four notes to sing "crooked," but he sustains at one tone the word "straight." When he sings of the rough places becoming a plain, a wide expansive vista opens to our view. He takes us to high places to see the spaces open before us, but in concluding he takes us back down to earth, and leaves us on a note of confident finality, while the orchestra continues to utter the jubilation the announcement has left in the heart.

The chorus takes up the theme of the revelation of God's glory. This is for all people, all flesh, and the combined voices sing it "together." It is as Amos had said:

> The lion has roared;
>   who will not fear?
> The Lord GOD has spoken;
>   who can but prophesy?
>
> (Amos 3:8)

## 5. BASS RECITATIVE

Thus saith the Lord of Hosts: Yet once, a little while, and I will shake the heav'ns and the earth, the sea and the dry land, and I will shake all nations, and the desire of all nations shall come.

The Lord, whom ye seek, shall suddenly come to his temple, ev'n the messenger of the Covenant, whom ye delight in; behold he shall come, saith the Lord of Hosts.

## 6. Bass Aria

But who may abide the day of his coming, and who shall stand when he appeareth? For he is like a refiner's fire.

## 7. Chorus

And he shall purify the sons of Levi, that they may offer unto the Lord an offering in righteousness. *(Haggai 2:6-7, modified; Malachi 3:1-3)*

And the people did return. Not all did; some of the Jews elected to stay in Babylonia. They were born there, they had business interests there, they saw no reason in traipsing across the country to an impoverished land simply because their parents and grandparents had come from there. Babylon for them was home, and in centuries to come, after the Jewish War of the second century A.D. scattered the Jews of Palestine and before the advent of Islam in the seventh century, Babylonian Jewry would be the center of gravity of the Jewish world.

But that is another story. Our interest is with those Jews, eager to reclaim the land promised to their ancestors, who went with Ezra and Nehemiah to start over again in their ancestral homeland. Some of those who returned were old enough to remember the old country and the splendor of Solomon's Temple. They had been among the deportees.

The prospect of return was more exhilarating than the fact. The land was depopulated, the economy depressed, and the site of the Temple was the heap of ruins that Micah, two hundred years earlier, had predicted it would become. To reclaim their heritage, the returned exiles would have to rebuild the Temple. To many the return proved a grievous disappointment. The work of rebuilding a whole society was daunting.

Here is where Haggai comes in. It is the words of this lesser known prophet of the restoration period that the bass takes up in the recitative. We know little about Haggai. The book of his oracles is short — two chapters. All the contents probably date from the year 520.

It was in 538 that Cyrus of Persia, conqueror of Babylon, decreed that all the captive peoples might return to their own lands. As Ezra gives his version of the edict, the Jews were encouraged to rebuild their Temple. But as late as 520, no particular progress had been made.

But the Temple had to be rebuilt, and worship purified. This is the burden laid on Haggai's heart by the Lord of Hosts ("hosts" originally referred to "armies"). It is an action the people must carry through, but it will at the same time be an action of God himself, as God describes the new Temple as a shaking of the universe. "I will shake the heavens and the earth, the sea and the dry land; and I will shake all nations."

Inhabitants of those regions were thoroughly familiar with earthquakes, when the very ground on which they stood could rise and ripple with terrifying destructive force. It provided a ready metaphor to describe the appearance of God — a theophany as scholars call it. We are told that when Moses went up on the mountain where he was to receive the Torah from the hand of God, the mountain quaked (Exodus 19:18). The judge Deborah, in her ancient song, recalls the image:

> The mountains quaked before the LORD,
> the One of Sinai,
> before the LORD, the God of Israel.
>
> (Judges 5:5)

One of the psalmists also makes use of the theme:

> O God, when you went out before your people,
> when you marched through the wilderness,

the earth quaked, the heavens poured down rain
at the presence of God, the God of Sinai,
at the presence of God, the God of Israel.

(Psalm 68:7-8)

Later the evangelist Matthew will underscore the significance of the death of Jesus the Messiah by telling us that when he yielded up his spirit, the earth shook (Matthew 27:51).

As the Hebrew poets tell of the quaking of Sinai, it is as a manifestation of the God of Israel, their national God. Haggai sees more. This shaking will encompass the whole cosmos that God spoke into being on the first three days of creation: the skies, the earth, the oceans, the continents. And it will be felt not only by Israel, but by all the world's nations. This theophany, this appearance of God, will confront all humanity.

"And the desire of all nations shall come." Here the Hebrew text presents us with a problem. The subject of the sentence can be read as a singular: "that which is precious, to be desired"; or as a plural: "treasures, valuables." Since the verb is plural, grammar dictates that the subject be understood as plural. This makes the sentence read, "The treasures of all nations shall come" — that is, come into the Temple which is to be constructed. Most translations render the sentence something like this. It is the Temple that Haggai is thinking of, and when he pictures its being built as an event to convulse the earth, he sees all nations bringing their wealth into its treasury. The text goes on to say, though omitted in the libretto of the oratorio, "and I will fill this house with splendor. . . . The silver is mine, and the gold is mine, says the LORD of Hosts." The prophet is using a material image to bring out what the exilic Isaiah had said:

Turn to me and be saved,
all the ends of the earth!
For I am God, and there is no other.
By myself I have sworn,
from my mouth has gone forth in righteousness

16

a word that shall not return:
"To me every knee shall bow,
    every tongue shall swear."

(Isaiah 45:22-23)

The apostle Paul will take up this theme in hymning the lordship of Jesus the Messiah:

so that at the name of Jesus
    every knee should bend
    in heaven and on earth and under the earth,
and every tongue should confess
    that Jesus Christ is Lord,
    to the glory of God the Father.

(Philippians 2:10-11)

The actual words of the prophet Haggai were not referring to the Messiah, but to treasures being brought into the Temple, but the two themes are concordant. The shaking of the world at the advent of the Messiah reorders the religious geography as all the nations respond to the divine summons. It is as Micah had said:

In days to come
    the mountain of the LORD's house
shall be established as the highest of the mountains,
    and shall be raised up above the hills.
Peoples shall stream to it,
    and many nations shall come and say:
"Come, let us go up to the mountain of the LORD,
    to the house of the God of Jacob;
that he may teach us his ways
    and that we may walk in his paths."
For out of Zion shall go forth instruction,
    and the word of the LORD from Jerusalem.

(Micah 4:1-2)

The recitative now shifts to the oracle of another prophet of the restoration period, Malachi, author of the last book of the Christian Old Testament. Malachi the person is unknown. Malachi was probably not even his name. The word means "my messenger," and may well be derived from use of the phrase in 3:1. Many believe that the book is an anonymous addition to the collection of the prophetic books.

Though we do not know the man and may not even know his name, we do know when he lived and what he thought. His message presupposes that the Temple has been rebuilt, and he is concerned that the worship of God conducted there be done properly and appropriately. His words probably come from the early fifth century.

In the passage immediately preceding the one used as the text for the recitative, the prophet has accused the people of wearying God. Malachi is not the first prophet to use the bold image of a God who has become exasperated with the worship of his people. Isaiah of Jerusalem had God depict the people coming to worship as a noisy trampling of his courts, because he could not tolerate solemn assembly that went along with iniquity. "I have had enough," he says (Isaiah 1:11-13). Amos, that most bitterly ironic of the prophets, had God speak of hating their solemn assemblies, or refusing to listen to their hymns until such time as justice should roll down like waters, righteousness like an everlasting stream (Amos 5:21-24). But all of that was before the exile, before the day of the Lord's judgment against his people. Now we are in a restored land, a reconstructed Jerusalem, and in a rebuilt Temple. Things should be different. But once again a prophet takes up the theme of God's weariness in putting up with his people: they are at it again.

The basis of the divine exasperation is a bit different now, in this later community. Earlier the people had conducted their usual rituals of worship while tolerating the social evils in the country, as if the God of Israel had no particular interest in how people were treated. In the restored Israel there is an agnostic strain in their thinking. They see evil around them (thinking of the hard times that they themselves are forced to undergo) and charge God with having no interest in redressing wrong. "Where is the God of justice?" they ask (Malachi 2:17). If God is so concerned with justice, if he cares so much for his people — or if such a God even exists — where is he? Why does he not appear and do something? If he is just, why does he not do something just? If he cares, why does he not do something caring? This is what Malachi, in the passage just preceding our text, accuses the people of thinking.

And then comes the answer to their questions. "The Lord whom you seek will suddenly come to his temple." They seek the God of justice; they will get him. He will come, come to the Temple itself. But when he does come, this God in whom they claim to take such delight, he will appear as a messenger of the covenant.

The covenant, a fundamental biblical idea, was the figure which Israel used to describe her relation with God. It was Israel's constitution, enacted on Mount Sinai with Moses. There God laid down the terms by which he would be Israel's God and Israel would be his people. The Ten Commandments are the opening words of the covenant, and indeed, its distilled essence. It was this covenant that the prophet Nathan had accused David of breaking in his affair with Bathsheba. David was to learn that the king was not above the law, since Israel's law was covenant law, laid down by God himself. It was the terms of the covenant that the old prophets had accused the people of breaking. When Hosea spoke of God's continuing wooing love for his faithless people, it was in terms of God's persistent fidelity to his side of the covenant.

What Malachi does is remind the people that the covenant has not been abrogated. The Lord is still their God and they are still his people, whether they like it or not. The demands of the covenant — as well as its promises — are still in force. Malachi's words, his response to the question, "Where is the God of justice?" are words both assuring and threatening. Both assurance and threat are underlined as the prophet repeats: "Behold he shall come, saith the Lord of Hosts."

As the singer continues with Malachi's pronouncement in the aria, we recall Amos ironically taunting the people for expecting the Day of the Lord, the day of God's victory over his enemies, hardly counting on the possibility that when that day should come, the Lord might count his own people among his enemies:

Alas for you who desire the day of the LORD!
    Why do you want the day of the LORD?
It is darkness, not light;
      as if someone fled from a lion,
      and was met by a bear.

(Amos 5:18-19)

So Malachi asks, "But who can endure the day of his coming, and who can stand when he appears? For he is like a refiner's fire." The biblical text goes on to describe him as being like laundry soap. The image is appropriate in the biblical context, but Jennens wisely omits this reference in the libretto.

This is the threat. Any age, any nation that thinks the God of justice is absent has a surprise in store — the terrifying prospect of his appearance! Yet his coming in judgment is not annihilating, but *refining*. It is to separate the good from the bad, so that the good may shine more brightly. Sin is always there to be dealt with. Malachi's Day of the Lord puts its emphasis not on the judgment brought to sinners, though that is assumed, but on the purification of God's people, especially as represented in the priesthood, the sons of Levi.

The twelve sons of the patriarch Jacob were the eponymous ancestors of the twelve tribes of Israel (Jacob's name was changed to Israel). Levi was one of those sons, and one of the tribes that constituted the nation. When the Hebrews conquered the land of Canaan and divided the country among the twelve tribes, Levi received no allotment. This was because the Levites' inheritance in the land was to be not land itself, but the service of the Lord. The Levites were to be the priests.

Malachi, like prophets before him, saw the faithlessness in the land to be a result of the faithlessness of the priesthood. In 2:2 he charged, "But you have turned aside from the way; you have caused many to stumble by your instruction; you have corrupted the covenant of Levi." But now, he says, this great shaking, this appearance of the Lord of Hosts in his Temple, this restatement of the covenant, this refinement of Israel's precious substance, will take the form of a renewed priesthood, the purification of the sons of Levi, so that they might once again be fit to bring offerings to the Lord on behalf of the people. Bringing offerings "in righteousness" means bringing them properly, in the right manner. The whole nation is in view, but the priesthood is in focus.

In the New Testament, the writer of Hebrews pictures Jesus the Messiah as our great High Priest, who has made an acceptable offering once and for all on our behalf. He was one who was like us in every respect, "so that he might be a merciful and faithful high priest in the service of God, to make a sacrifice of atonement for the sins of the people" (Hebrews 2:17).

The evangelist Luke tells us of an occasion when the Holy Family, soon after the birth of Jesus, is in Jerusalem. They encounter in the Temple an aged man named Simeon, to whom the Holy Spirit had revealed that he should not die until he had seen the long-awaited Messiah. Inspired by the Spirit, Simeon went to the Temple. When he saw the infant Jesus, he took him in his arms and said:

> Master, now you are dismissing your servant in peace,
>     according to your word;
> for my eyes have seen your salvation,
>     which you have prepared in the presence of all peoples,
> a light for revelation to the Gentiles
>     and for glory to your people Israel.
>
> (Luke 2:29-32)

In the Temple the priests made offerings on behalf of the sins of the people. Malachi sees God manifesting his presence there once again, affirming his covenant by convulsing the universe in an action that will call all nations to respond to the call of Israel's God. In the Temple the infant Messiah is hailed as the revelation to the Gentiles. The writer of Hebrews uses the image of priesthood, sacrifice, and Temple to tell of the Messiah's work among us, taking away the sins of the world.

THE BASS opens the recitative with the ominous prophetic prelude: "Thus saith the Lord of Hosts." The musical line trembles with the word "shake," as the line rises to the heavens and then down to the earth. There is more reverberation on "shake" until it is resolved with the surprising message that "all nations" are involved, on three simple descending notes. When the promise begins, that "the desire of all nations shall come," the music slows and grows warmer to let us absorb the message, the line cadencing with firm assurance in F major. But immediately following this cadence a shift to G minor ushers in Malachi's remaining words, recited with sure strength, and the recitative comes to a close with the confident prophetic signature with which it began: "saith the Lord of Hosts."

The aria is questioning, challenging: When he does appear, will you be able to survive the experience? His coming is like a refiner's fire; the music glows red and leaps like the flames in the refiner's furnace.

The purification of the Levites, the priesthood, is the climax of Malachi's oracle, and as the climax of this sequence in the oratorio, the chorus sings the promise. Here are the people joining together in the exultant hope of being rendered fit to come before God, of being brought before the Lord by the ministrations of the Messiah as our great High Priest, to whom these words, in the context of the oratorio, point.

## 8. ALTO RECITATIVE

**Behold, a virgin shall conceive, and bear a son, and shall call his name Emmanuel, "God with us."** *(Isaiah 7:14; cf. Matthew 1:23)*

These are the words of Isaiah of Jerusalem, spoken sometime during the years 734-733 B.C. In almost any modern translation, the word "virgin" does not appear, but rather, "young woman," "maiden," or the like. There is a simple reason for this. That is what the Hebrew text means. There is a word for "virgin" in Hebrew, but it is not used here. The word Isaiah chose indicates a sexually mature young woman, but with no focus on her sexual experience or lack of it.

Here is the story. Ahaz was King of Judah. Just to the north in the neighboring kingdom of Israel, which had come into being two hundred years earlier after Solomon's death, when the northern tribes rebelled against the House of David, Pekah was king. Further north, Rezin was king of Syria. And to the east, in the northern Mesopotamian valley, the fierce Tiglath-Pileser was King of Assyria, a warlike empire intent on subjugating the smaller states along the Mediterranean. Pekah and Rezin had entered into an alliance against the Assyrian monarch, and challenged Ahaz to join. Ahaz believed the three of them together stood no chance against Assyrian arms and wanted no part of it. On the other hand, Pekah and Rezin were threatening him if he did not join, and Ahaz was terrified at the prospect of losing such a contest.

But the Lord had no intention of allowing these two minor kings to conquer Jerusalem, and so indicated to the prophet Isaiah. The prophet arranged to encounter the king and gave him God's assurance that he had nothing to fear from the alliance of Israel and Syria. God even volunteered to give Ahaz an assuring sign, and allowed him to name it: "Ask a sign of the LORD your God; let it be deep as Sheol [the land of the dead] or as high as heaven" (Isaiah 7:11). But Ahaz put on a show of piety. Had not Moses said that one should not put the Lord to a test? (Deuteronomy 6:16). "I will not ask, and I will not put the LORD to the test" (Isaiah 7:12). Losing patience, Isaiah then announced that God would give him a sign whether he liked it or not, but the sign would give no present assurance. It would be something that would not be manifest until later.

Hear then, O house of David! Is it too little for you to weary mortals, that you weary my God also? Therefore the Lord himself will give you a sign. Look, the young woman is with child and shall bear a son, and shall name him Immanuel. He shall eat curds and honey by the time he knows how to refuse the evil and choose the good. For before the child knows how to refuse the evil and

23

choose the good, the land before whose two kings you are in dread will be deserted. (Isaiah 7:13-16)

This then is the sign. Somewhere in the land there is a young woman who is pregnant (or possibly will become pregnant; the Hebrew can be argued at this point). When her child is born, the political situation will have completely changed. There will be no more threat from Pekah and Rezin. In thanksgiving, the woman will be able to name the child Immanuel, which means "God is with us." Before the child is old enough to know right from wrong, Syria and Israel will be wiped off the map.

We do not know who the young woman was. Some suggest that she was the wife of Isaiah, some suggest the wife of the king. She need not be anyone in particular. The point is that Isaiah tells the king that in no more than nine months he will learn the truth of what God has been trying to tell him. The prophet was speaking to the king in a particular historical situation, about something the king was going to live to see unfold. He was not speaking about something centuries in the future, which could hardly have been much of a sign for a worried king. There is no reference to a virgin birth. The virgin birth is a specifically Christian doctrine; it was never a feature of the Jewish messianic hope. The only references to it in the Bible are in Matthew 1 and Luke 1.

But at the beginning of Matthew's gospel, after Joseph has been assured by an angel that he should not hesitate to marry his pregnant fiancée Mary, we are told that her miraculous conception took place to fulfill Isaiah's words, as Matthew quotes them:

"Look, the virgin shall conceive and bear a son,
    and they shall name him Emmanuel,"
which means, "God is with us."

(Matthew 1:23)

And in this case, "virgin" accurately translates the Greek word Matthew uses.

Here is the story. In the third and second centuries before

Christ, a translation of the Hebrew Scriptures into Greek was made by Jewish scholars resident in the metropolitan city of Alexandria in Egypt. They chose to translate Isaiah's word by the Greek word *parthenos,* which does mean "virgin," or at least can mean that. The semantic range of that word is wider than that of our word "virgin." We do not use the word in any sense other than a technical one, to refer to a person's lack of sexual experience. But the Greek word could be used less specifically. A group of girls walking down the street might be called *parthenoi* quite comfortably, without any interest in their sexual histories. The word was not an altogether inappropriate choice on the part of the translators.

When the Christian movement began, its literature was written in Greek, the universal second language of the eastern Mediterranean at the time. Hebrew, Coptic, Syriac, to some extent even Latin, were local languages. Only if something were written in Greek could it hope to enjoy a circulation beyond linguistic boundaries. So the first Christian writers wrote in Greek. When they had occasion to quote Jewish Scripture, they often quoted it from this Greek translation.

The evangelist Matthew quotes Scripture far more than any other gospel writer. He wants to tie down everything he can to a fulfillment of prophecy. This citation of Isaiah 7:14 is the first of many such references. Matthew tells us of Mary's miraculous conception, and then tracks it down to prophecy by quoting these words from the Greek translation, which lent themselves beautifully to his purpose. To be sure, the original sense of the words are not quite as appropriate, but this is hardly the only time in the New Testament that Old Testament words are quoted from the Greek translation to prove a point that the original Hebrew would not support. The translators of the King James Version were well aware of this, as they indicate in their preface, in a section where they are defending the use of a variety of English translations:

> No cause therefore why the word translated should be denied to be the word, or forbidden to be current, notwithstanding that some imperfections and blemishes may be noted in the setting

forth of it. . . . The translation of the Seventy (the Greek translation) dissenteth from the Original in many places, neither doth it come near it, for perspicuity, gravity, majesty; yet which of the Apostles did condemn it? Condemn it? Nay, they used it.

Nonetheless, there is a certain harmony between Isaiah and Matthew's use of him. Both speak of a coming deliverance. Isaiah was speaking of a sign of deliverance from two threatening kings. Matthew is referring to deliverance from sin, which is why he has just said that Mary's child would be named, not Immanuel, but Jesus. "Jesus" is an Anglicized form of the Greek form of the Hebrew name Joshua, which means "the Lord saves." Jesus is in fact never called Immanuel in the New Testament, but Matthew will refer back to that prophetic name and its meaning in the last verse of his gospel, when Jesus takes his departure from his disciples with the words, "And remember, I am with you always, to the end of the age" (Matthew 28:20). "God is with us . . . I am with you." With these assurances Matthew envelops his gospel.

Handel's librettist could not have known all this, of course, but it doesn't really matter. The oratorio is a Christian telling of the story, with the virgin birth of the Messiah taken for granted. In the context of the oratorio, the passage as quoted from the King James Version (with the addition of the words "God with us") is quite fitting. Here, for the first time in the work, the birth of Jesus the Messiah is specifically referred to.

～

AFTER THE CHORUS has exultantly rejoiced at the promise of renewed and purified access to God, the music becomes quiet, as the alto virtually whispers to us the promise of the prophet. It does not come in earthquake, in flame, or in wind, but as Elijah discovered the word of God, in a still, small voice (I Kings 19:11-12). The alto introduces the announcement with "Behold." This same word, sung over the same interval and in the same key, will recur later in the oratorio when the bass tells us of another mystery, that of the resurrection: "Behold, I tell you a mystery." The musical identity is highly appropriate, for like the resurrection of the dead, the virgin birth is a mystery. Not a riddle or puzzle for which we can find some explanation or solution, but a mystery, before which we can only come in the kind of awe communicated by the alto's soft assurance that in this mystery, God is with us.

### 9. Alto Aria and Chorus

**O thou that tellest good tidings to Zion, get thee up into the high mountain, O thou that tellest good tidings to Jerusalem, lift up thy voice with strength, lift it up, be not afraid, say unto the cities of Judah: Behold your God!** *(Isaiah 40:9, KJV margin)*

**O thou that tellest good tidings to Zion, arise, shine for thy light is come, and the glory of the Lord is risen upon thee.** *(Isaiah 60:1, modified)*

A flashback to the exile. At the beginning of the oratorio we listened to the words of the exilic Isaiah, speaking for God to his deported nation: "Comfort my people. . . ." That particular passage ended with the chorus singing that the glory of the Lord was about to be revealed.

Now we return to that passage in Isaiah 40, but here we are transported to the other end of the Fertile Crescent from Babylonia, to Jerusalem itself. Here is the lonely city who mourns and is mourned in the five despondent dirges that constitute the chapters of the book of Lamentations:

How lonely sits the city
   that once was full of people!

(1:1)

From daughter Zion has departed all her majesty.

(1:6)

Zion stretches out her hands,
  but there is no one to comfort her.

(1:17)

This is the forsaken city whom the faraway exiles remembered with a desperate affection:

If I forget you, O Jerusalem,
  let my right hand wither!
Let my tongue cling to the roof of my mouth
  if I do not remember you,
if I do not set Jerusalem
  above my highest joy.

(Psalm 137:5-6)

Zion and Jerusalem are technically separate, but in the devices of Hebrew poetry they designate the same entity: the beloved city. Originally Zion may have referred to the oldest part of the city, the ancient Canaanite stronghold captured by David and known as the City of David. Later the term was transferred to the Temple mount, the area north of the old city into which Jerusalem expanded under Solomon and where he built the Temple. It is in any case a considerable elevation, about 2500 feet above sea level, but not the highest point in the vicinity. In spite of this, however, in Hebrew poetry one always travels up to Jerusalem, from whatever direction or height, since figuratively, if not in fact, it is "the highest of the mountains . . . raised above the hills" (Isaiah 2:2; Micah 4:1).

To understand the structure of the oracle now being sung, we must observe that the text of the oratorio omits three verses between "the mouth of the Lord hath spoken it" and the beginning of this aria, "O thou that tellest good tidings." The opening admonition was to comfort God's people. The prophet then proceeds with three stanzas indicating how this comfort is to be effected. First is the promise of the highway across the desert for the Lord and his train to go in glory back to the homeland. Second, in 40:6-8, is the omitted section in which a voice cries that human life is as transient as grass, but that although all living things fade away like wild flowers, the word of God will stand forever.

The third specific instruction to comfort are the words of the prophet's third stanza, verses 9-11, which are the opening lines of this musical section. The libretto reads the translation in the margin of the King James Version rather than the text itself. (Like recent versions, the translators of the King James provided an abundance of marginal notes giving alternate translations; unfortunately they are seldom included in editions of the Bible today.) The text reads, probably more accurately, "O Zion, that bringest good tidings. . . . O Jerusalem, that bringest good tidings." The one who bears the good tidings may be Jerusalem itself, speaking to the cities of Judah. The reason for this difference in understanding is technical. The one Hebrew word that is translated "thou that tellest good tidings" is feminine (in Hebrew verbs as well as nouns are inflected for gender). If a person is intended, it is a woman, but since no such person is in view, and since the city is customarily personified as a woman, it seems that the King James text and some modern versions are correct in reading the passage in such a way as to make Jerusalem the herald, not the one to whom the good tidings are to be spoken. But some modern versions prefer the understanding found in the libretto, and it is quite possible that the text before us is correct. It is certainly justifiable, and is surely appropriate in the context of the oratorio.

Here is the picture. The bereft city sits lonely, her people many decades long departed. Then, from a high mountain in the distance appears a herald, a forerunner of the regal caravan proceeding westward across the wilderness. The city looks up expectantly and hears the proclamation of the good news: Your God is on his way back! Here he comes!

Zion, Jerusalem itself, is of course a mountain. The Psalmist describes it as "His holy mountain, beautiful in elevation" (Psalm 48:2). But now this city set on a hill looks to higher elevations to hear the glad news proclaimed. The herald may shout fearlessly aloud, not only to the Holy City but to all the habitations of surrounding Judah, that the new day has arrived, that the Lord God is coming in all his might, bringing his people with him (Isaiah 40:10, omitted in the oratorio).

As Handel has used this passage, however, we are not speaking about exiles returning from captivity, led by their God. The good news is being shouted out to us, God's people sitting as lonely and deserted as old Jerusalem, that our God is on the way. The oratorio's reference is to the advent of Messiah, whose birth by a virgin mother has just been announced. In the coming of the virgin's son, God himself is manifest among us. This is good tidings indeed, what the New Testament calls "gospel," a word which means "good news" and which translates a Greek word meaning precisely that.

We are not yet finished with Isaiah 40. We will return to it in section 20, "He Shall Feed His Flock."

The aria continues by shifting to Isaiah 60:1, which appropriately refers back to 40:5, "and the glory of the LORD shall be revealed." Zion is still being addressed; the verbs are still feminine. The city is pictured as a woman cast down to the ground.

> Fallen, no more to rise,
>  is maiden Israel;
> forsaken on her land,
>  with none to raise her up.
>
> (Amos 5:2)

> Rouse yourself, rouse yourself!
>  Stand up, O Jerusalem,
> you who have drunk at the hand of the LORD
>  the cup of his wrath.
>
> (Isaiah 51:17)

The prostrate one is commanded to rise, to shine, to glow with the reflected light from the dawn breaking upon her, to shine as the face of Moses shone from his encounter with God on Sinai. The glory of the Lord has come up over the mountains like the break of day, "the light of the gospel, the image of the glory of Christ, who is the image of God" (II Corinthians 4:4).

Then your light shall break forth like the dawn,
   and your healing shall spring up quickly;
your vindicator shall go before you,
   the glory of the LORD shall be your rear guard.

(Isaiah 58:8)

~

MUSICALLY, we are following here the same structure as in the previous two sequences: a recitative, followed by an aria, followed by a chorus — a sequence in which there is a progression of thought following through the three parts. By following this well-established structure here, Handel joins these verses from different parts of Isaiah. After the quiet mystery of the recitative, announcing Messiah's coming birth, the aria is vivified with the happy announcement of the birth itself. Ascending lines dominate; the melody comes downward only so as to rise again. In the phrase, "lift up thy voice with strength, lift it up, be not afraid," one can sense the urging of the prostrate Jerusalem to rise: get up, get up! On "be not afraid" it is as if Zion has risen to her feet, ready to make the strong and fearless proclamation, "Behold your God!" The aria ends with the line rising to heights reflective of the light of God's glory.

There should be no pause between the aria and the chorus; the choir should be standing and ready to take up without missing a beat. The enthusiasm, the joy of the dawning light of glory must not flag. Unlike in the previous two choruses, this time the united voices have nothing more to add by way of text; the alto's words are simply repeated. But this is the risen Jerusalem singing for joy; this is Zion shining in the light of the risen glory. And she makes her proclamation with strength indeed, and without fear. Once more the people join in affirming the words of the prophet.

**For behold, darkness shall cover the earth, and gross darkness the people: but the Lord shall arise upon thee, and his glory shall be seen upon thee, and the gentiles shall come to thy light, and kings to the brightness of thy rising.** *(Isaiah 60:2-3)*

"Let there be light" (Genesis 1:3). Thus does the Lord God, in the first chapter of the Bible, begin speaking the universe into existence. But this young light is light quite apart from any physical source. The sun, the moon, the stars do not come into being until later in the week of creation, on the fourth day. Thus the writer teaches that the true source of genuine light is not those heavenly bodies, but God the creator himself. The same idea is echoed in the last chapter of the Bible as well, when, speaking of the saints of God in Heaven, the seer of Revelation writes: "And there will be no more night; they need no light of lamp or sun, for the Lord God will be their light, and they will reign forever and ever" (Revelation 22:5). So does Jesus the Messiah speak in the Gospel of John: "I am the light of the world. Whoever follows me will never walk in darkness but will have the light of life" (John 8:12). John the Evangelist works constantly throughout his book with the images of light and darkness; early on, before introducing Jesus into the narrative, he identifies him with the real light: "The true light, which enlightens everyone, was coming into the world. He was in the world, and the world came into being through him; yet the world did not know him" (John 1:9-10). "God is light and in him there is no darkness at all" (I John 1:5).

The bass begins his recitative by continuing the words of Isaiah 60 into verses 2-3. He describes the world before the coming of the true light, the Messiah. It is in darkness — gross darkness. All the peoples of the world — and that is what is meant by "the people" in this passage — are enshrouded in its folds. But as for you, Zion, the Lord shall arise upon you like dawn — the same as "the glory of the Lord" in verse 1, sung earlier by the alto and the chorus — and you will reflect his glory.

The imagery of God's coming expressed in terms of light, fire, and other natural phenomena is much older than this prophet. We have already seen it in the Song of Deborah (Judges 5), and we find it in Psalm 18:7-15, in a vivid depiction of God's appearance as a convulsing of nature. But as Isaiah 60 employs the imagery, something is different. Those earlier theophanies took place against a setting of battle, or warfare. It is David's military victories over his enemies that are being celebrated in the language of Psalm 18. Deborah pictures the stars in their courses fighting against her opponent (Judges 5:20). But here all warlike elements are dissolved. After all, the prophet has said of Jerusalem that "her warfare is accomplished." Now the victory of God, his glorious appearing, functions to bring light, not only to his own people, but to all nations.

This last portion of the book of Isaiah, chapters 40–66, is convinced that Israel has a responsibility to the rest of the world.

> I am the LORD, I have called you in righteousness,
>> I have taken you by the hand and kept you;
> I have given you as a covenant to the people,
>> a light to the nations.
>
> (Isaiah 42:6)

> I will give you as a light to the nations,
>> that my salvation may reach to the end of the earth.
>
> (Isaiah 49:6)

These words will be quoted by the apostle Paul when he preaches the Messiah at Antioch of Pisidia (Acts 13:47) and before King Agrippa (Acts 26:23). So does old Simeon rejoice as he holds the infant Jesus in his arms:

> for my eyes have seen your salvation,
>> which you have prepared in the presence of all peoples,
> a light for revelation to the Gentiles
>> and for glory to your people Israel.
>
> (Luke 2:30-32)

The rising of the light on Zion comes as an illumination for the world. "The Gentiles shall come to thy light, and kings to the brightness of thy rising." This, incidentally, is probably the source of the legend that the magi who visit the infant Jesus in Matthew 2 were kings. The Bible does not say that — but in reflection on this passage and others such as Psalm 68:29 and 72:10 the legend grew and transformed the magi into kings. (The King James Version refers to them as "wise men"; one of the meanings of the phrase "wise man" in King James' day was one who practiced occult sciences.)

~

THE MUSIC of the recitative is dark, slow, and heavy. It lowers, ponderous with "a darkness that can be felt," like the darkness that came over Egypt on the night of the death of the firstborn (Exodus 10:21). But as the light begins to dawn the music rises and becomes expansive, conveying the light that has risen upon Zion to shine upon the world, the light of the Messiah, that shines into the darkness, and which the darkness has never extinguished (John 1:5).

## 11. BASS ARIA

**The people that walked in darkness have seen a great light. And they that dwell in the land of the shadow of death, upon them hath the light shined.** *(Isaiah 9:2, modified)*

The Bible thus begins with the creation of light and ends with the establishment of light eternal for the servants of God in Heaven. In between is the story of salvation, the story of God's coming to us, of his bringing light into our darkness, darkness which we have chosen rather than light, because our deeds are evil (John 3:19).

The aria now sung by the bass continues the theme of the recitative by reflecting on the words of the earlier Isaiah of Jerusalem, the prophet who had pronounced the Immanuel oracle. In the literary context in Isaiah, this passage follows a development from that earlier oracle of 7:14, set during the time of conflict between King Ahaz and his enemies to the north. Ahaz was unmoved by Isaiah's assurances, by the prophet's insistence on neutrality in the impending conflict between Israel and Syria on one side and Assyria on the other. And so to extricate himself from his immediate threat, Ahaz appealed for assistance to Tiglath-Pileser of Assyria.

Isaiah could see it coming. Assyrian forces would inundate Syria and northern Israel; he could see the tide pouring into Judah and lapping at the gates of Jerusalem itself.

> The Lord is bringing up against it the mighty flood waters of the River, the king of Assyria and all his glory; it will rise above all its channels and overflow all its banks; it will sweep into Judah as a flood, and, pouring over, it will reach up to the neck; and its outspread wings will fill the breadth of your land, O Immanuel. (Isaiah 8:7-8)

The last exclamation is wonderfully ambiguous. On the one hand it reaches back to the Immanuel oracle of the previous chapter, the birth of the child named "God is with us." On the other hand it can be heard here as a cry of despair, "God be with us!" The name may be construed either way. But even though the tribes of the north would be lost, Isaiah believed that God would protect Judah, the land ruled by the son of David. He calls on the distant countries to observe what will happen and stand dismayed:

> Take counsel together, but it shall be brought to naught;
> speak a word, but it will not stand,
> for God is with us.
>
> (Isaiah 8:10)

Immanuel. The name is once again the promise of Judah's security.

Tiglath-Pileser was more than willing to accommodate King Ahaz' plea for help. Westward he came, through Syria, through

Israel, marking the end of the history of the northern tribes. Exiled here and yon, their people vanished from history, assimilated into the nations. The future of the people then rested with Judah alone, looking to her king, the son of David, for protection. Isaiah was once again right. The Assyrian armies penetrated Judah, laying siege to Jerusalem, but they did not succeed. The city remained untaken. God was with them. Immanuel.

The prophet could see nothing but willful faithlessness about him. The clearest assurances were of no avail; the soundest counsel yielded to folly. The people resorted to sorcerers and mediums and magicians rather than repairing to the Lord, to whom Isaiah called them. He had done his best: "Bind up the testimony," he declares, "seal the teaching among my disciples. I will wait for the LORD, who is hiding his face from the house of Jacob, and I will hope in him" (Isaiah 8:16-17). There can be no dawn for such an obdurate people.

They will pass through the land, greatly distressed and hungry; when they are hungry, they will be enraged and will curse their king and their gods. They will turn their faces upward, or they will look to the earth, but will see only distress and darkness, the gloom of anguish; and they will be thrust into thick darkness. (Isaiah 8:21-22)

And so do people live, groping and cursing in a darkness of their own choosing. But Isaiah's God will not leave them in darkness. He is intent on coming to them with light. The next chapter begins with an affirmation of a reversal: "But there will be no gloom for those who were in anguish" (Isaiah 9:1). There follows what may possibly be an editorial comment from one of the compositors of the book, to the effect that while the lands of Zebulun and Naphtali (two of the northern tribes, here representing defunct Israel) were once brought into contempt, the time would come when God would make that territory glorious: "the way of the sea, the land beyond the Jordan, Galilee of the nations" (Isaiah 9:1).

Let the evangelist Matthew make the transition from that

statement to verse 2, the text of the aria. Matthew uses these two verses to introduce the ministry of Jesus. Jesus has been baptized and has bested Satan in the wilderness. He leaves his hometown of Nazareth and moves to Capernaum, a city by the Sea of Galilee, in what had once been the tribal territory of Zebulun and Naphtali. This, he says, was to fulfill Isaiah's words:

> Land of Zebulun, land of Naphtali,
>> on the road by the sea, across the Jordan, Galilee
>>> of the Gentiles —
> the people who sat in darkness
>> have seen a great light,
> and for those who sat in the region and shadow of death
>> light has dawned.
>>>>>>> (Matthew 4:15-16)

The gospel writer pictures the light dawning for the world when Jesus the Messiah begins his ministry. In the context of the oratorio, the light dawns with the birth of Jesus the Messiah.

And in the context of Isaiah's prophecy, that light dawns because of something that has happened, a historical event that portended a new chance for the nation. We do not know precisely what that event was. The life situation has been swallowed by the literary context in which the words are preserved. It may well have been the birth of a crown prince. It may have been the accession of a new king. In either case, it is likely that the person in question was good king Hezekiah, who succeeded Ahaz on the throne of David. And it is of this event that the chorus is about to sing.

⁓

THE MUSICAL LINES of the aria well picture the subject matter. The music is painful; it gropes. It moves hesitantly, like one reaching about in the dark for something solid. Its angular lines reflect confusion and disorientation. But all this ends with solid footing finally found: "upon them hath the light shined."

## 12. Chorus

**For unto us a Child is born, unto us a Son is given, and the government shall be upon his shoulder, and his name shall be called: Wonderful, Counsellor, The Mighty God, The Everlasting Father, The Prince of Peace!** *(Isaiah 9:6)*

Israel had always avoided a kingship until Saul was anointed. The antimonarchical party in Israel feared their becoming like other nations. God was their king. If they were to be ruled by an earthly king, they would soon be indistinguishable from other peoples. In many respects, what they feared eventually did come true.

The states of the ancient Near East had a wealth of traditions surrounding their traditional kingships. From land to land they differed, but there were common elements. There was songcraft and poetry to serve on various occasions of state: enthronements, royal weddings, and births in the royal family. And there was always a connection of some kind of the king with the gods. The kingdom of Israel did indeed learn from the precedents in other nations. Psalm 72 is obviously a song written by some court poet for a royal wedding; the original occasion is now lost, but surely it was often used over the centuries of the kingdom's life. Psalms 2 and 110 sound very much enthronement psalms, composed for use on the ceremonial accession of a new monarch. Psalm 2 refers to the king as the son of God, adopted, as it were, on the day of enthronement. The king there confesses: "He said to me, 'You are my son; today I have begotten you'" (Psalm 2:7).

This language used of the king should not be surprising when we consider that as early as the covenant with David in II Samuel 7, Solomon is specifically spoken of as the son of God.

He shall build a house for my name, and I will establish the throne of his kingdom forever. I will be a father to him, and he shall be a son to me. When he commits iniquity, I will punish him. . . . (II Samuel 7:13-14)

38

Nor should it be surprising when we realize that the phrases "son of . . ." or "daughter of . . ." are quite often used as figures of speech in Hebrew, to indicate a person or even a thing possessing characteristics associated with someone or something else. "Son of God," then, when used of the reigning king, did not indicate for the Israelite any mythological idea or actual descent from deity, but simply that in some respects — majesty, strength, might — he shared characteristics with God. When Psalm 29 calls on the "sons of gods" to ascribe glory and strength to the Lord, the psalmist may well be thinking of earthly rulers (Psalm 29:1).

Isaiah may well have been a court poet, a kind of poet laureate called on at some occasion to compose a poem appropriate for the birth of a prince or the accession of a king, say Hezekiah. The verses now sung by the chorus, Isaiah 9:6, are part of such a poem or song.

At first reading the psalm does sound very much like the celebration of a birth in the royal household. But given the imagery of Psalm 2, of God's "begetting" the king as his son, probably at the enthronement, it is quite possible that Isaiah wrote this piece for Hezekiah's ceremonial accession to the throne. This would have been an occasion of national jubilation. A new chance. Isaiah is hopeful it will bode well for the nation. This is why the people who have been walking in darkness have seen a great light, for a child is given us this day to be our ruler: "the government shall be upon his shoulder." The new prince, or king, is given a series of four divine titles. There was precedent for this outside Israel and within. Consider David's noble titles: "Son of Jesse . . . the man whom God exalted, the anointed of the God of Jacob, the favorite of the Strong One of Israel" (II Samuel 23:1).

The new ruler is to be "Wonderful Counsellor" (the comma between the two words in the King James Version is a mistake). Perhaps this means "he who plans wonders." He is to be "Mighty God," a figure of speech for "godlike in might," "divine hero." He is to be called "Everlasting Father," not meaning that he is immortal, but that his paternal care for his people is perpetual. He is to be the "Prince of Peace," of *shalom,* meaning much more than that he is a ruler who brings cessation of warfare. He is also one who brings in the reign of all of what that pregnant Hebrew word means: prosperity, health, virtue, peace, all aspects of a positive life. Though omitted in the text of the oratorio, the oracle goes on to say:

> His authority shall grow continually,
>     and there shall be endless peace
> for the throne of David and his kingdom.
>     He will establish and uphold it
> with justice and with righteousness
>     from this time onward and forevermore.
>
> (Isaiah 9:7)

These are Messianic words. They pertain to the Anointed One, the King. The prophet himself was not peering centuries into the future to predict Jesus' birth; he saw no further than Hezekiah. But he read into Hezekiah's coming the messianic hope, the hope of a ruler worthy of David, the hope that would eventually survive the extinction of the kingship itself in 587 B.C., the hope that nourished Jewish expectation for the future, the hope that was vibrant wherever and whenever oppressed Jewry looked for divine deliverance, the hope that was still very much alive when Jesus conducted his ministry.

Strangely enough, this oracle of Isaiah is never quoted in the New Testament, nor is Jesus ever referred to by any of the divine titles ascribed to the messianic ruler in this passage. Yet in Christian faith, Jesus is the ultimate fulfillment of Isaiah's prophecy, and it is not wrenching a verse from context to see it so. The verse rests squarely in the middle of the biblical highway across the wilderness that leads to God's salvation of humanity. The prophet spoke then and there of hope for a national renewal and salvation that he himself might see. But in the themes he uttered and the notes he struck, he was speaking far more. He was describing the one further down that road, the one indeed to whom the road leads, the one who would say to his disciples just before he left them: "All authority in heaven and on earth has been given to me" (Matthew 28:18). This passage, known as the Great Commission, closes the book of Matthew. Its last words are "And remember, I am with you always, to the end of the age." So Matthew envelops his gospel with the promise of God's presence, beginning with the Immanuel oracle (1:23). Just as Jesus is never referred to by any of the royal titles of our passage, he is never called Immanuel either, but when the gospel ends with Jesus' utterance "I am with you always," Matthew makes it clear that he is our Immanuel, our sign that God is with us. The name of the young woman's son and the royal titles of the Judean kings all reverberate at the sounding of the name of the Virgin's Son, the Son of God. The Messiah has come! And this is what the chorus celebrates.

~

HERE IS one of the high moments of the oratorio. It is the people again who join together in joy over the birth of the royal child, exhilarating in the titles of the one whom they adore. Handel plagiarized the music from one of this own operas (much of the music of *Messiah* was originally written for other purposes), but with the exception of making the simple conjunction "for" bear altogether too much weight, at few places in the work do text and music work together more sympathetically than here. We have reached a climax in the structure of the oratorio. The recitation of prophecy has been building up to this moment, Messiah's birth and the prospect of deliverance, of salvation.

## 13. PASTORAL SYMPHONY

Let us pause in the pasturelands of a Judean evening and, with the shepherds, await the coming of Messiah.

Many Jews today — perhaps it is fair to say most — no longer look for the advent of the Messiah as a person. There have been so many opportunities for God to act, chances such as the Holocaust, and still Messiah has not come. The concept has thus been reinterpreted. If the whole idea is not simply relegated to the sphere of religious history, it is now taken to refer not so much to the Messiah as a person as to the nature of a Messianic age. Indeed, from a Jewish point of view, much of the lore surrounding the coming Messiah is postbiblical. The biblical passages that are messianic in nature speak as much, if not more, of the messianic age of peace as they do of Messiah himself (see Isaiah 11:1-9).

Among the Orthodox, however, the expectation remains alive. Messiah will come in God's good time and restore the Davidic kingdom. The Temple will once again be built, sacrifices will once again be offered, and Israel may once again observe Torah as God delivered it to Moses.

Not even in ancient Israel did all Jews await a Messiah. The Sadducees had little use for the idea. On the other hand, the Pharisees and their followers among the common folk did cherish and nurture the hope. Wherever, whenever there was oppression, there bloomed the expectation that the Kingdom would return to Israel. From time to time actual messianic movements did arise around some particular person. The Jewish historian Josephus, a younger contemporary of Jesus, tells about a Theudas who persuaded his followers to gather up their belongings and go with him to the Jordan River, where he was going to part the waters miraculously. The Roman governor, learning of it, sent out the cavalry. Many of the group were killed, and others taken prisoner. The governor understood that this was no ordinary group of religious fanatics; this was a messianic movement and hence a threat to Roman rule. This Theudas is mentioned in Acts 5:36-37, along with a similarly fated Judas the Galilean. In the second century some of the leading Jews hailed Simon Bar Kochba as Messiah, but his uprising met a similarly disastrous end.

One must remember what the Jews of Jesus' day were looking for. Then we see why many did not accept Jesus as the Messiah: he did nothing Messianic. He did not, in fact, overthrow Rome and restore the Kingdom of David. Far from it, he died an ignominious death. The Messiah was to be victorious. A suffering Messiah was a contradiction in terms.

Jesus does appear to have been a popular figure, at least in the early months of his ministry. No doubt many people did leap to the hope that here at last was God's Messiah. At least one (Simon the Zealot) and probably two (Judas Iscariot) of his own disciples were drawn from the political terrorists devoted to ridding the land of Roman rule. But Jesus does not openly claim to be the Messiah and appears somewhat embarrassed by the implication that he is. In Mark 1:21-28 he silences a demon who recognizes him as the Holy One of God. At a central point in that gospel, 8:27-30, Peter at long last confesses Jesus as the Messiah, but when Jesus then begins speaking of his coming suffering, Peter reveals that he understands nothing. A suffering Messiah cannot be. John tells of an incident following the feeding of the thousands, when Jesus realizes that the people there on the lakeside are about to proclaim him king. He is in a corner. He must either declare himself or deny it. He must make his rebellious move or lose his following. He withdrew (John 6:15). Later in the same chapter, John tells us that his popular following abandoned him (John 6:66).

Jesus is arrested on the charge that, like Theudas, he represents a threat to Roman rule. In all four gospels, Pilate asks Jesus point-blank: "Are you the King of the Jews?" In all four gospels, Jesus gives an enigmatic reply: "You say so." Those are your words, not mine (Matthew 27:11; Mark 15:2; Luke 23:3; John 18:33, 37). Earlier, when Jesus is examined by the High Priest, three of the evangelists have the High Priest ask Jesus the bald question: "Are you the Messiah?" The answer varies. In Matthew he replies with his response to Pilate: "You say so" (26:63-64). In Luke he evades the questions (22:67-68). Only in Mark (14:61-62) does Jesus give a simple answer: "I am."

But Mark (and Matthew as well) tell of a revealing incident that takes place a few days earlier, during Jesus' last week (Mark 14:3-9; Matthew 26:6-13). Jesus is a dinner guest at the home of a man who lives just outside Jerusalem. During the meal, an unnamed woman appears carrying a container of very expensive ointment. She breaks the seal on the jar and pours the ointment on Jesus' head (not so strange a thing; a host might do this for an honored guest). Jesus was now literally anointed. Hers was a messianic action. But

Jesus does not upbraid her or tell her to be quiet. Some there do blame her for wasting such a precious commodity: it could have been sold and the proceeds given to the poor. But Jesus, now the literal Anointed One — Messiah — defends her. But he reinterprets the figure. Kings were not the only ones anointed. Dead bodies were also anointed as part of the funeral preparations. And Jesus says, "She has anointed my body beforehand for its burial." The emphasis has been taken off the imagery of triumphant kingship and shifted to that of suffering and death.

When those Jews and Gentiles who confessed Jesus as the Messiah did so, they were reinterpreting the figure. True, Jesus did nothing messianic according to the traditional expectation. But he came, in lowliness and suffering, to release his people and all people from a bondage more confining that that imposed by Rome. He came to free us from our sin.

~

THE TEXT of the oratorio has led us from the gloom of the exile to the new hope of the restoration, exemplified in the coming of the glory of the Lord, the Messiah. We are now about to hear the announcement of Messiah's birth. It will be made this Judean evening to some shepherds. It is the only incident that is narrated in the entire musical work.

We must prepare for the announcement. We must remove ourselves from the jubilation of hearing the prophetic word and settle down on the quiet hillsides around the village of Bethlehem. We must prepare our hearts for the great Coming. We must humble ourselves with the shepherds. The Pastoral Symphony, the only instrumental interlude in the work, does this for us. The music is calm, and cool, and sweetly lyrical. It breathes the quietness we must experience before the great announcement is made.

## 14, 15, 16. Soprano Recitatives

There were shepherds abiding in the field, keeping watch over their flock by night.

And lo! the angel of the Lord came upon them and the glory of the Lord shone round about them and they were sore afraid.

And the angel said unto them: Fear not; for behold, I bring you good tidings of great joy, which shall be to all people. For unto you is born this day, in the city of David, a Saviour, which is Christ the Lord.

And suddenly there was with the angel a multitude of the heav'nly host, praising God, and saying:

## 17. Chorus

Glory to God in the highest, and peace on earth, good will towards men! *(Luke 2:8-11, 13-14, modified)*

The text is from the Gospel of Luke. Only Luke tells us of the shepherds' story, but it is typical of this gospel writer. No other evangelist is so insistent on the concern of Jesus for the poor, the outcast, the lowest strata of society. The very first words of Jesus' ministry that Luke records are his reading in the synagogue from the Isaiah scroll: "The Spirit of the Lord is upon me, because he has anointed me to bring good news to the poor" (Luke 4:18). When Luke's Jesus delivers the Beatitudes, he will not say, "Blessed are the poor in spirit" (Matthew 5:3), but "Blessed are you who are poor" (Luke 6:20). He will not say, "Blessed are those who hunger and thirst for righteousness" (Matthew 5:6), but "Blessed are you who are hungry" (Luke 6:21). In keeping with this motif Luke sets the announcement of Messiah's birth. It comes not to kings or sages, but to poor people. In one ancient Jewish tradition, shepherds were notoriously untrustworthy, because they were so poor as to be forced to steal. But David himself had been a shepherd boy, and in those very same hills. God himself was praised as the Shepherd of Israel in Psalm 23, and the evangelist John will have Jesus presenting himself as the good shepherd, who lays down his life for his sheep (John 10:11). The Messiah as King must have a people, just as the shepherd has a flock. The prophet Ezekiel speaks of this: "I will set up over them one shepherd, my servant David, and he shall feed them: he shall feed them and be their shepherd" (34:23). The Latin word for shepherd is "pastor."

A rich imagery combines here in this tale. The ancient world was not without its fanciful notions of idyllic pastoral scenes involving shepherds, just as we find in romantic English literature that draws from such sources as Virgil. To Handel's audience the mention of a pastoral symphony and an appearance of shepherds probably suggested such ideas, but in Luke's biblical text there is something earthy, laborious, and sweaty. These are poverty-stricken, hardworking people out in that field, spending the pasturing season with no roof over their head. (One Greek word is translated "abiding in the field"; it does not mean that the shepherds happened to be outdoors that night, but rather they were living there. Their home was with their sheep.)

Luke's mention of the shepherds living in the fields is the only clue the Bible gives us as to the time of year when Jesus was born, and it is only a slim clue. Usually the flocks went out to pasture in March or April and came back in November. The tradition that Jesus was born on December 25 does not come, then, from the Bible, but it can be traced back as far as the fourth century.*

---

* We really do not know why this date was chosen. Perhaps, as some suggest, in the Christianization of the Empire this Christian feast day took the place of the Saturnalia held on December 25. Perhaps, as others suggest, it was because this was the date of the winter solstice in the ancient calendar. From this date on, the daylight lengthens. This would be supported by the observation that a fourth-century tradition still observed in the church celebrates the birth of John the

46

The shepherds were "keeping watch," literally translated "watching watches" (the day was divided into twelve hours; the night was divided into four watches). Elsewhere in the land that night other people were keeping their watch. Watch was being kept in the Temple. Watch was being kept at the ruler's palace. But it was to the poor folk in the hill country keeping night watches over a flock of someone else's livestock that the angel appeared. They were the first to hear the good news. It was on them, not the priests, not the rulers, that the glory of the Lord shone.

"And lo!" "Lo" does not appear in modern translations since the Greek word it translates is not found in the oldest and best manuscripts of this verse, but it is frequent in the New Testament as either "Lo" or "Behold." It is used well over 200 times; virtually every occurrence is in the narrative literature of the Gospels, Acts, and Revelation. It is not really a Greek usage, but a Semitism, an imitation in Greek of Old Testament diction. Hebrew has a very common word, *hine,* which has no real semantic content. It is an attention-getter: Now hear this! Hey! Look here! Sometimes it seems to have the stylistic function of shifting the point of view from that of the omniscient narrator to that of a participant. When the Scriptures were translated into Greek, the translators, having no equiv-

---

Baptist on June 24, the ancient date of the summer solstice, after which daylight dwindles. John the Baptist said of Jesus: "He must increase, but I must decrease" (John 3:30). According to Luke, the conception of Jesus took place six months after the conception of John the Baptist (Luke 1:26). Yet another suggestion is that since creation was thought to have taken place on the first day of spring (March 25 at the time of Jesus), it would be appropriate to think of that as the day of Jesus' conception, with his birth nine months later on December 25. But the reasons are lost. We do not know.

Nor does our text actually say that Jesus was born at night, though it leaves that impression. The tradition that Jesus was born at midnight comes from the Wisdom of Solomon, a book included in the Catholic Bible but not considered canonical by Jews or Protestants. Wisdom 18:14 is actually talking about the night of the first Passover, when Egypt lay quiet while the angel of death came to do his work, but the words were easily appropriated to refer to Jesus, who in the Gospel of John is the Word of God. The text reads: "For while gentle silence enveloped all things, and night in its swift course was now half gone, your all-powerful word leaped from heaven, from the royal throne. . . ."

alent Greek word, used an imperative form of the verb "to see." New Testament writers, infusing their narrative with a biblical aura, adopted the usage; hence the common English translation "Behold." "Lo" may have had an archaic sound even by the time of the King James Version in 1611; "behold" is used far more frequently. The same distribution is found in Shakespeare. Actually, "lo," from Middle English, is a fairly close equivalent to the Hebrew word.

An angel appears ("the" angel is a mistranslation). Just what Luke envisaged in writing this is hard to say. The Greek word, as well as the Hebrew word translated "angel" in the Old Testament, is the common noun meaning "messenger." The root of the word is the same seen in "evangel," "gospel, good news." In the oldest strata of the Old Testament, God sometimes speaks directly to human beings and sometimes speaks through a "messenger." Occasionally the narrative varies as to just who is speaking, God or a messenger (Judges 6:11-18). These messengers who appear to deliver a message from God were apparently thought of as having human form. The angel of the Lord who announces the birth of Samson to his mother and father is referred to by both as a "man of God" (Judges 13). In Genesis 18 three men are entertained by Abraham at a meal; one of them is the Lord and the other two are angels, messengers. Or are all three angels? In Genesis 32:22-32 Jacob wrestles with a man who mysteriously shows up from nowhere (and who turns out to be God), but when Hosea refers to the incident he calls Jacob's opponent an angel (Hosea 12:4).

God is often pictured in the Old Testament as a king. Since earthly kings had royal courts, it was natural to extend the analogy to picture a heavenly court around God. I Kings 22:19 pictures "the Lord sitting on his throne, with all the host of heaven standing beside him." It is presumably to his courtiers that God speaks, "Let us make humankind in our image" (Genesis 1:26), and, referring to the people laboring to build the tower of Babel, "Come, let us go down, and confuse their language" (Genesis 11:7). These may be the "sons of God" who intermarried with human women in Genesis 6:1-2, or who came to present themselves before the Lord in Job 2:1.

So far we have the idea of God sending messengers to speak

his word to human beings, and the idea of God the King surrounded by a heavenly court. To this we must add the cherubim and seraphim. A cherub (cherubim is plural) was a fanciful creature, familiar in ancient Near Eastern art, composed of parts of several animals: perhaps a human head, with the body of an ox or a lion, but always winged. Cherubim appear often. They guard the entrance to Eden in Genesis 3:24. God rides through the sky mounted on a cherub (Psalm 18:10). Cherubim are a decorative motif on the Ark of the Covenant, the chest in which the tables of the Ten Commandments were deposited (Exodus 25:18-20). Ezekiel gives an elaborate description of the cherubim he sees in his initial vision (Ezekiel 1:5-14; 9:3; 10:1-15). Seraphim (seraph is singular) appear only once. The term means "flaming ones." Isaiah sees a vision of seraphim attending God on his throne. We are told only that they had six wings. Both cherubim and seraphim are pictorial descriptions of the holy majesty of God. Neither is referred to as angels.

This is as far as the Old Testament goes, but in the Jewish literature produced after the exile, books such as I Enoch, Jubilees, and the Testaments of the Twelve Patriarchs, there is elaborate speculation about the angels of God. They are arranged in celestial hierarchies, pictured as an army (more of this later), as messengers from human beings to God as well as from God to people. The idea even develops of evil angels. Many of the angels receive names. The angel Raphael appears in the late book Tobit, which is included in the Catholic Bible.

All this later lore about angels was taken for granted by most Jews in the New Testament period, and hence in the New Testament itself. It is specifically the angel Gabriel who announces the conception and birth of Jesus to Mary in Luke 2.

The translators of the Hebrew Scripture into Greek, in the pre-Christian centuries, simply rendered the Hebrew word "messenger" by the Greek word "messenger," *angelos*. It was about this time that much of the Jewish speculation about angels was taking place. When in the late fourth century the great Jerome translated the Bible into Latin, he did not use the Latin word for "messenger." Now perceiving these beings as supernatural entities of a special nature, he simply transliterated the Greek word as *angelus*. Hence a specialized term has been taken over, and used in English, to describe what in the Old Testament are simply God's messengers. Christian tradition is replete with angelology, but most of its sources are extrabiblical. Traditions about the divine messengers, the heavenly court, the winged creatures about the throne of God have combined with the luxuriant speculation of the intertestamental period. In the Bible the angels symbolize God's holiness, his majesty, and his communication with the human world. It is probably safe to say that most popular thinking about angels and picturing of them owes more to John Milton and to Doré's illustrations for Milton's epics than to the Bible.

An angel appeared to these shepherds; they are being confronted with God's message, and they are illuminated with the divine light of his effulgent glory. Their reaction is fear, a consistent response in the Bible to the presence of God.

In the phrase "sore afraid," "sore" is an archaic term meaning "very, extremely." It is cognate with the German *sehr*, "very."

Well might they fear. God is holy; that which was holy was dangerous. The Ark of the Covenant was holy; one would die on touching it. The garments of the priests were holy; the people had to protect themselves from their contagion (Ezekiel 44:19). When Jacob realizes that he has met God, he exclaims, "I have seen God face to face, and yet my life is preserved" (Genesis 32:30). But Hosea saw that the presence of God with Israel was more than a threat; it could also be a source of good: "I am God and no mortal, the Holy One in your midst, and I will not come in wrath" (Hosea 11:9).

The angel's first word is a quelling of fear, which is God's word to a humanity suddenly stricken before a sense of the divine. In Genesis 15:1 and again in 26:24, God encounters Abraham, and his first words are "Fear not." When, in Judges 6:22-23, Gideon realizes that he has been speaking with an angel, he cries, "Help me, Lord GOD! For I have seen the angel of the LORD face to face." God reassures him "Peace be to you; do not fear, you shall not die."

This word from God goes on to counter great fear with great joy. This is the content of the good news — gospel — that the angel is about to announce: joy. Joy is another characteristic theme in Luke's gospel. Indeed, it frames the gospel. Here, at Jesus' birth, the angel announces great joy to the shepherds. In the closing verses of the book (24:52-53), the disciples, after receiving Jesus' blessing before he ascended into heaven, return to Jerusalem with great joy, blessing God, just as these shepherds after visiting the infant Jesus, will return to the fields glorifying and praising God (Luke 2:20).

This is a great joy "which shall be for all people." Luke uses a relative pronoun here which is not the usual choice. This particular word imparts a qualitative aspect to the statement: "the kind of joy which will be for all people" (it is possible to read too much into this, but the text is capable of this interpretation). "All people" is probably a misinterpretation, although an attractive one. Luke's choice of vocabulary rather clearly points to Israel; he literally says "all the people," and the word for "people" which he chooses is usually used of the Jews in distinction from others. In spite of Luke's desire to make his Jesus relevant for the Gentile world, this application to Israel makes sense. The shepherds are Jews, they are among those who await Messiah's coming, and his coming is the content of the proclamation.

"This day" is a favorite phrase of Luke's; counting the book of Acts, which is from the hand of the same author, he uses it twenty times. It carries with it a sense of fulfilled expectation, a sense of the ultimate concretized in time and space. When Jesus reads from Isaiah in the synagogue in Nazareth, he sits down and announces — and this is also Luke's announcement to the reader: "Today this Scripture has been fulfilled in your hearing" (4:21). When Jesus speaks forgiveness of sin to the paralyzed man and heals him, the onlookers exclaim, "We have seen strange things today" (5:26). Before his arrest, Jesus tells a spluttering, protesting Peter, "I tell you, Peter, the cock will not crow this day, until you have denied three times that you know me" (22:34). He tells the repentant criminal on the adjacent cross: "Truly I tell you, today you will be with me in Paradise" (23:43). As the angel pronounces the words, a sense is conveyed that the long-awaited time has arrived. It is now here.

The City of David is, of course, Bethlehem. The phrase has two meanings in the Bible. Sometimes it refers to the old part of Jerusalem, that part of the city which was settled when David captured it from the Canaanites, but here it refers to David's hometown, about five miles south of Jerusalem (it is now part of the larger urban complex). The angel could, of course, simply have uttered the name of the town, but it is important to make the connection with David. This is the Messiah's birth — the one who will restore the promises made to David.

"Savior" as a title for the Messiah is somewhat unusual in the New Testament, compared with the more frequent titles Lord, Messiah, Son of God, and Son of Man. In the Old Testament it is used of military heroes who deliver their people (II Kings 13:5; Nehemiah 9:27), but more frequently, particularly in Isaiah, it is used of God: "For I am the LORD your God, the Holy One of Israel, your Savior" (Isaiah 43:3). Many of the New Testament references also have specific reference to God. In the gospels, only Luke and John use the title of Jesus, each only once. In the letters ascribed to Paul where we can be certain of Paul's authorship, the title occurs only in Philippians 3:20: "But our citizenship is in heaven, and it is from there that we are expecting a Savior, the Lord Jesus Christ." Paul uses it in the sense of a deliverer to come at the end time. Other references to Jesus as Savior occur in books that are probably among the latest of the New Testament books to be written. It appears that the title did not catch on at first, but was only gradually adopted. Probably the reason for this is that the term was often used in Greco-Roman popular religions, particularly in the cult of the Emperor, who was hailed as "god and savior." The earliest Christians may have avoided the term to dissociate their worship from pagan practice.

The one born today is indeed the Messiah — Christ — the first time the word has been used in the oratorio. And he is the Lord. Luke refers to Jesus quite often as Lord. Like John, he is not hesitant about its use in referring to the earthly Jesus. Matthew and Mark are much more sparing. It is an important word, and it is ambiguous. On the one hand, it was the ordinary title of polite address to a man: "Sir." It often means that in the gospels. But to both Jew and Gentile it had a broader reference. By the time of Jesus, the Hebrew name of God, Yahweh (Jehovah, anglicized), had become too sacred to pronounce, and whenever it was encountered in the reading of Scripture, the phrase "the Lord" was substituted. (This is reflected in English translations of the Old Testament. Whenever the word appears in capitals, LORD, it is the translators' signal that this is not what it says. It reads "Yahweh," God's proper name, but ancient tradition is being followed in substituting "the LORD.")

To the Jew, then, the word could denote God himself. In the Gentile world, the term could be used of savior figures of popular cults, and thus also potentially denoted deity. For a Jew to hail Jesus as Messiah did not make the person any less a Jew. Such a confession might well mark a person as eccentric, but not heretical. To confess, however, that Jesus is Lord, was virtually to equate him with God, and burst the bounds of Jewish orthodoxy. It was very likely this confession which eventually marked the young Christian movement as more than another Jewish sect, but a religion in its own right, which by the end of the first century it had clearly become. It is a climactic and central confession of the Christian faith. Paul looks to the day when every tongue will "confess that Jesus Christ is Lord, to the glory of God the Father" (Philippians 2:11).

As the apostle looked for the day when mortal tongues would confess Jesus as Lord, we now hear the tongues of angels praising God. On the mention of Christ the Lord there suddenly — immediately — appears a multitude (literally, a "fullness") of the heavenly host (literally, "a heavenly army").

In Section 5 we heard the bass sing of the "Lord of Hosts." "Hosts" here is fundamentally, or at least originally, a military term. Hosts are armies (I Samuel 17:45). The ascription goes back to the days of the military conquest of Canaan, of Saul and David leading the armies of Israel into battle. "The LORD is a warrior; the LORD is his name" (Exodus 15:3). But the term is eventually transferred to groups of angels. "Jacob went on his way and the angels of God met him; and when Jacob saw them he said, 'This is God's camp!'"

(Genesis 32:1). In I Kings 22:19, the host of heaven around God's throne are clearly angels. Further, the phrase can be used of the stars. This is presumably the reference when Jeremiah speaks of the people's apostasy in worshiping "the sun and the moon and all the host of heaven" (Jeremiah 8:2).

Perhaps we are to think here of the angel's being suddenly joined by an immense choir of other angels; perhaps we are to think of the angel's being accompanied by the vast array of the constellations and galaxies: "when the morning stars sang together, and all the heavenly beings shouted for joy" (Job 38:7). Whatever the picture, a newly beheavened earth now reverberates to the massive song.

"Glory to God in the highest" does not mean "in the highest way, superlatively," but rather, "in the highest places," that is, in heaven itself. The contrast here is between heaven and earth. God's glory must be hymned in heaven, and the blessings of God's domain, focused as "peace," *shalom* comes down to earth. The song, as quoted in Handel's text from the King James Version, is in a tripartite form:

Glory to God    in the highest
Peace    on earth
goodwill    to men.

In modern translations there is universally a bipartite structure, with words to the effect:

Glory  to God    in the highest
Peace   on earth   among those with whom he is pleased

The New Revised Standard Version is typical:

"Glory to God in the highest heaven,
and on earth peace among those whom he favors."

One will notice that the parallel structure of the lines is cleaner in the second form than in the King James form. That is important, for this kind of parallelism between lines is a central organizing feature of Semitic poetry. But that is not the real reason for the striking difference in translation. The modern translations are reading a different Greek text than that used by the translators of 1611, a text almost universally recognized today as more original. Strikingly enough, the only difference in the Greek of these two readings is the presence or absence of one letter. Without a sigma at the end of the word translated "good will," the King James Version is correct. With the sigma — and there are good but technical reasons for believing it belongs — "peace on earth, good will to men" becomes literally "peace on earth to men *of* good will." The good will intended is not human, people who show good will to others; it refers rather to God's good will, God's good pleasure. There is precedent in the Dead Sea Scrolls for this interpretation.

Here the host of heaven sing of glory and peace on the occasion of the Messiah's birth. When Jesus makes his triumphal entry into Jerusalem on the week of his crucifixion, Luke will have the welcoming crowds echo the song of the angels: "Blessed is the King who comes in the name of the Lord! Peace in heaven and glory in the highest heaven!" (19:38).

~

ACCOMPANIED by only a few chords, the soprano quietly begins telling the story, a soaring line arching across the night sky. But now the music shimmers and rustles with the dazzling light of God's glory and the whirring wings of angels, as we hear of the appearance of the angel and the shepherds' fear. But again, the soprano goes without accompaniment to make the announcement; the world must listen silent and breathless to the news. Then again the whirr of wings as the angelic host appears. The chorus sings the angelic song. Up to this point, the chorus has represented the people's affirmation and expansion of the soloist's preceding words. Here they are the angels, but yet, the people also. This is our song, as in the words of the carol, "the whole world send back the song which now the angels sing."

After the soprano's recitative, there was no aria. This breaks with the previous pattern, but here there is no time for the luxury of an extended aria. After the announcement is made, we must immediately hear heaven and earth resounding with the good tidings. The aria will wait for the angels to finish. Then the soprano will draw conclusions from what has happened.

## 18. Soprano Recitative

**Rejoice greatly, O daughter of Zion, shout, O daughter of Jerusalem, behold, thy King cometh unto thee. He is the righteous Saviour, and he shall speak peace unto the heathen.** *(Zechariah 9:9-10, greatly modified)*

This exultant song looks backward and harks forward; it remembers and anticipates. It will be helpful here to quote the entirety of the passage from the King James Version, for the librettist has omitted some lines helpful for understanding the context, and has taken liberties with the text elsewhere:

> Rejoice greatly, O Daughter of Zion;
> Shout, O Daughter of Jerusalem;
> behold, thy King cometh unto thee:
> he is just, and having salvation;
> lowly, and riding upon an ass,
> and upon a colt the foal of an ass.
> And I will cut off the chariot from Ephraim,
> and the horse from Jerusalem,
> and the battle bow shall be cut off;
> and he shall speak peace unto the heathen:
> and his dominion shall be from sea even to sea,
> and from the river even to the ends of the earth.
> (Zechariah 9:9-10)

The words look back to the dying Jacob, with his sons gathered around his deathbed to receive their father's paternal blessing. To

Judah, ancestor of David, he says, "The scepter shall not depart from Judah . . . and the obedience of the peoples is his. Binding his foal to the vine and his donkey's colt to the choice vine . . ." (Genesis 49:10-11).

The last chorus sang the words of the angels, anticipating the acclaim of the crowds welcoming Jesus into Jerusalem, and these words from the prophet Zechariah are focused on the same event. When Jesus enters the city, he rides on a donkey, and in telling of the event, three of the evangelists, Matthew, Mark, and John, will quote these words.

The book of Zechariah, like Isaiah, is divided into two parts, the last of which, chapters 9–14, is a collection of anonymous prophecies. Our text here may be as late as the fourth century, from the time of the coming of Alexander the Great into the Holy Land.

The prophet tells of the coming of the messianic King. He calls on Zion, Jerusalem, to break out into singing (in the Hebrew figure of speech, the "daughter" probably *is* Jerusalem or Zion), because her king is on the way. We recall the opening sections of the oratorio, with the prophet bidding the people of Jerusalem to prepare for the Lord's coming; we recall the alto's aria summoning Zion to shout the good tidings to all the land that God, their light and glory, is on the verge of appearing. Now the Holy City is called to song celebrating his birth.

The phrase "He is the righteous savior" has been altered by the librettist, and it has proved a somewhat difficult line for all translators. The Hebrew reads, "He is righteous and saved." This is indeed the reading of the Geneva Bible of 1560, the version that commanded the devotion of the English-speaking peoples before the King James Version: "He is just and saved." The ancient Greek translation, as well as Jerome's Latin Bible, rendered the passive form "saved" as an active, "saving." The King James straddles the issue with its awkward and ambiguous "having salvation."

But the Hebrew is probably right. The Messiah is first of all righteous: "The days are surely coming, says the LORD, when I will raise up for David a righteous Branch, and he shall reign as king and deal wisely, and shall execute justice and righteousness in the land" (Jeremiah 23:5). "See, a king will reign in righteousness, and princes will rule with justice" (Isaiah 32:1). But righteousness in the Bible carries the idea of vindication, of having been declared — by God — to be in the right; for the source of all righteousness, even Messiah's, is God. As the psalmist sings, "Give the king your justice, O God, and your righteousness to a king's son. May he judge your people with righteousness, and your poor with justice" (Psalm 72:1-2).

And the coming king is "saved," delivered from his enemies, vindicated by God, although in this context there is no idea of military victory. God again is the source of all deliverance. The Revised English Bible puts it well: "See, your king is coming to you, his cause won, his victory gained. . . ."

That line will be omitted by the gospel writers in telling of Jesus' triumphal entry, for in that context, the winning of his cause, the gaining of his victory, still lies ahead, though only by a few days. The ancient reader of those gospels, familiar with Zechariah's words, would note the omission and anticipate the fuller manifestation of the prophet's pronouncement at the resurrection.

King Messiah, in the revelation of his glory, will proclaim peace — the fullest blessings of divine *shalom* — to the nations of the world. "Heathen" is not a good choice of words. The Hebrew word refers to non-Jewish peoples and does not have here the derogatory meanings associated with our word "heathen." The word originally referred to people inhabiting the heaths — wild, uncultivated land, just as the word "pagan" originally referred in Latin to dwellers in the remote countryside. Both words came to be used in English to refer to peoples who were neither Jewish, Christian, nor Muslim — that is, those who did not worship the one God. But as England expanded its imperial reach into the "pagan" world and the English became aware of "pagan" customs, the peoples came to be branded with the opprobrium of Christian revulsion against much in these alien cultures, and both words, "heathen" and "pagan," took on such negative connotative freight that they can no longer be used in a technical sense.

It is to all the world, at any rate, that Messiah speaks peace.

Symbolic of it is his riding upon a donkey. On the one hand, we hear several times of Israelite rulers riding donkeys. The Song of Deborah refers to "you who ride on white donkeys" (Judges 5:10), and we hear of two of the Judges whose descendants rode donkeys (Judges 10:4; 12:14). David himself, fleeing Jerusalem to escape his rebel son Absalom, goes with donkeys (II Samuel 16:1). On the other hand, horses were associated with warfare: "In that day, says the LORD, I will cut off your horses from among you and destroy your chariots" (Micah 5:10). "Alas for those who go down to Egypt for help and who rely on horses . . ." (Isaiah 31:1). This messianic king comes in humble fashion, riding a donkey as did the Israelite princes of old, not riding above the heads of his people on a war horse. The prophet is clear about this: it is a donkey, the foal of a donkey — not that it need be a young animal, but that it is pure-bred. There is no horse in its ancestry.

Messiah has come, but an unexpected Messiah, one we may not be as willing to accept. He has not come to overthrow our political enemies. He comes to accept suffering on our behalf; that is how he will win his cause and gain his victory. And so the words of Handel's text, though not well representing the prophet's ancient words, speak truly, and speak of peace: "He is the righteous Savior." When Jesus enters the Holy City, mounted on the back of a donkey, the crowds cry out, "Hosanna!" The word means "Save us, we pray!" It is of this salvation at hand that Jerusalem is to sing.

~

AND IT IS an exuberant aria, with the soprano voice taking the jubilation to the highest registers. Rejoice! Rejoice! Two commanding notes, with the second coming to no musical resting place, but leaving a line unresolved; but the third, "Rejoice, O Daughter of Zion," turns cartwheels of joy. The summons is breathless: "Behold . . . thy king . . . cometh . . . un . . . to thee!" When the line is repeated it comes down in two-note steps as if we are being bid to bow our knees to the ground before the king. The line depicting the righteous savior's speaking peace to the nations is broad and expansive, as though the world were listening to the words earlier spoken to Jerusalem, "Your warfare is over — accomplished."

## 19. ALTO RECITATIVE

Then shall the eyes of the blind be open'd, and the ears of the deaf unstopped; then shall the lame man leap as a hart, and the tongue of the dumb shall sing. *(Isaiah 35:5-6, modified)*

## 20. ALTO ARIA

He shall feed his flock like a shepherd, and he shall gather the lambs with his arm; and carry them in his bosom, and gently lead those that are with young. *(Isaiah 40:11, modified)*

## SOPRANO ARIA

Come unto him all ye that labour, come unto him that are heavy laden, and he will give you rest. Take his yoke upon you, and learn of him, for he is meek and lowly of heart, and ye shall find rest unto your souls. *(Matthew 11:28-29, modified)*

## 21. CHORUS

His yoke is easy, his burthen is light. *(Matthew 11:30)*

Virtually all that is known of the Jesus of history, the man of Galilee, the teacher from Nazareth, is found in the four canonical gospels of the New Testament. In the remaining New Testament books, we find surprisingly little mention of this figure. There is a great deal about the risen Lord, the Lord Jesus Christ, but almost nothing about the earthly figure. Outside of the gospels, the only incident in his life of which we are told in any detail is his Last Supper (I Corinthians 11:23-35). Of his teaching, only one saying is recorded in the New Testament outside the gospels: "It is more blessed to give than to receive" (Acts 20:35). It is as Paul says, "Even though we once knew Christ from a human point of view, we know him no longer in that way" (II Corinthians 5:16).

Nor does Handel's *Messiah* focus on the earthly figure. Up to this point we have heard of the coming of the Messiah. Here, and into Part II, we have material reflective of the life, death, and resurrection of Messiah. From Section 37 of Part II and on to the end of the work, we hear of the reigning Lord and our own place in the eternal plan. Old Testament; Gospel; Epistle.

But in the entire scope of the work, only the three sections we now consider speak of the Lord's earthly ministry, of his work and words. And that is done by indirection. We are told of no incident, and he himself does not speak.

The alto opens with a passage from Isaiah. The two verses of the recitative, Isaiah 35:5-6, follow logically on the soprano's aria of the Savior's coming. The libretto does not include the preceding verse, 35:4, but that verse provides the transition: "Say to those who are of a fearful heart, 'Be strong, do not fear! Here is your God. He will come with vengeance, with terrible recompense. He will come and save you.'" The entirety of chapter 35 has been appropriately compared to a symphonic movement in sonata form. Verses 1-2 are a joyous celebration of a renewed world of nature breaking forth into song. The central section, 3-6a, is quieter, urging strength and courage and promising new hope. The finale, 6b-10, recapitulates the joy, returning us to the image of the highway through the desert for God's people to travel:

A highway shall be there, and it shall be called the Holy Way . . . it shall be for God's people. . . . And the ransomed of the LORD shall return, and come to Zion with singing; everlasting joy shall be upon their heads; they shall obtain joy and gladness, and sorrow and sighing shall flee away. (Isaiah 35:8-10)

It is in this context that the words of our text are uttered. Here is the glad announcement of a new thing. At the time of Isaiah's call experience, God had told him, "Make the mind of this people dull, and stop their ears, and shut their eyes, so that they may not look with their eyes, and listen with their ears, and comprehend with their minds" (Isaiah 6:10). The later Isaiah had asked, "Who is blind but my servant, or deaf like my messenger whom I send?" (Isaiah 42:19). But now there will be a reversal. Redemption is being proclaimed: sight to the blind and hearing to the deaf. Israel receives a new call to her mission as the people of God.

These words are used in the oratorio to tell of the ministry of Jesus, of his beneficent works, how he gave sight to the blind and hearing to the deaf, and made the lame walk. We do not see the afflicted people, we do not hear the Lord's healing words to them, nor is there any description of the resulting joy. It is all the culmination of prophecy. The God who has come down the long highway from exile, whose glory has risen upon us, who has entered his city in royal humility, has come to heal us of our afflictions. He has come as the righteous Savior. The Greek verb "save" is used in the New Testament far more frequently than the noun form "Savior." It can refer to rescue from physical danger. Usually it refers to salvation in the full theological sense, but it sometimes refers to the healing of disease. In Matthew 9:22 Jesus heals the woman with the hemorrhage; in Mark 10:52 and Luke 18:42 he heals blind men; in Luke 17:19 he heals a leper. In each case he says: "Your faith has saved you — healed you — made you whole."

While it seems natural language to speak of Jesus healing people, we do not usually use this word of modern doctors. Physicians cure people; they do not heal them. "Cure," from a Latin root meaning to care for, is reserved for a methodical and scientific approach to restoring health. "Heal," however, signifies "to make whole." Appropriately, we speak of wounds healing. Jesus' ministry is one of healing, not curing. He makes people whole. His healing activity becomes a fitting picture, an earnest, of the ministry of salvation. The librettist chose his text well.

John the Baptist, he who had stood on Jordan's bank and announced the Coming One, was in prison. He had heard news of Jesus' activities, but he had heard nothing to confirm his belief that Jesus was to be the Messiah. Where was he gathering his army? Messiah was supposed to free the prisoners. Why, then, was John still behind bars? He sent a message to Jesus: "Are you the one who is to come, or are we to wait for another?" Jesus' response: "The blind receive their sight, the lame walk, the lepers are cleansed, the deaf hear, the dead are raised, and the poor have good news preached to them" (Matthew 11:2-5). He does not answer John's question. Only the eyes of faith can draw from these observations that Messiah is among us. And it is faith, Jesus tells the afflicted ones, that has brought about their healing — their salvation.

As the aria begins, we are reminded that "we are his people, and the sheep of his pasture" (Psalm 100:3). The alto's words return us, at this point near the end of Part I, to the same passage from Isaiah with which the oratorio began. It is a continuation of "Comfort ye my people," and of "O thou that tellest good tidings to Zion." This first part of the work will end on the note of comfort, the same theme it struck at the opening.

To picture God as a shepherd, a fairly familiar figure in the Old Testament, is to picture us his people as sheep. This is not a romantic image; it is drawn from the realism of livestock culture. It is not a picture of cuddly innocence. We are small. We are helpless against predators. We fall into rushing streams and are washed away. We wander away from the safety of the flock and the shepherd. We do silly things. But God is our shepherd, as the psalmist sings in Psalm 23. He feeds us until we have our fill; sheep do not lie down in green pastures unless they are satisfied. When he leads us to water it is not to the dangerous freshets cascading down steep rocky hillsides, but to quiet pools, where we refresh ourselves in safety. Even when we walk along the perilous cliffs, we have nothing to fear. Our shepherd is with us, keeping us from falling, warding off

the predators with his rod and staff. "Your rod and your staff —
they comfort me" (Psalm 23:1-4).

Without such a guide and guard, we are lost, "like sheep
without a shepherd," as Jesus thinks of the crowds who come from
all over to hear the good news and be healed of their diseases
(Matthew 35–36).

The exilic Isaiah spoke these words of the exiles returning
home. Just as Micah had foretold: "I will surely gather all of you,
O Jacob, I will gather the survivors of Israel; I will set them together
like sheep in a fold, like a flock in its pasture" (Micah 2:12). Just as
Jeremiah had foreseen: "He who scattered Israel will gather him,
and will keep him as a shepherd a flock" (Jeremiah 31:10).

It was Israel the prophet was speaking of, shepherded by their
God. But in the context of the oratorio, the words look ahead to
Jesus, who calls himself the Good Shepherd.

"I am the good shepherd. The good shepherd lays down his life
for the sheep. The hired hand, who is not the shepherd and does
not own the sheep, sees the wolf coming and leaves the sheep and
runs away — and the wolf snatches them and scatters them. The
hired hand runs away because a hired hand does not care for the
sheep. I am the good shepherd. I know my own, and my own
know me." (John 10:11-14)

This is what, in Part II, the Messiah will do for his own — lay
down his life for them. We are his people and the sheep of his
pasture. In his guidance there is safety. In his arms there is comfort.
In his flock there is salvation.

The New International Version puts it well: "He tends his flock
like a shepherd: He gathers the lambs in his arms and carries them
close to his heart; he gently leads those that have young."

The soprano's aria takes over from the alto by responding to
the prophet's words with the words of Jesus. These lines, and the
line of the following chorus, are the only words of Jesus used in the
libretto, and they are modified, so as to be cast in the third person.
The Messiah himself never speaks in the oratorio.

The saying is found only in the Gospel of Matthew. This gospel, like the three others, is quite anonymous, but tradition has ascribed it to one of the disciples of Jesus. The tradition may or may not be accurate — most scholars think it is not — but all agree that the book was written by a Jewish Christian learned in the traditions of Judaism. Some of these themes emerge in our present passage.

Jesus' words, "Come unto me," are echoing the words of Heavenly Wisdom. In the book of Proverbs, Wisdom is personified as a female figure who was with God in the beginning of creation (Proverbs 8:22-31), and who calls everyone to herself. "To you, O people, I call, and my cry is to all that live" (8:4). "Come, eat of my bread . . ." (9:5). In the book of Sirach (or Ecclesiasticus), another book from Israel's wisdom tradition, the author's closing chapter calls on humanity to come to wisdom. Wisdom speaks: "Come to me, you who desire me, and eat your fill of my fruits . . ." (Sirach 24:19). "Draw near to me, you who are uneducated, and lodge in the house of instruction. . . . Put your neck under her yoke, and let your souls receive instruction; it is to be found close by" (Sirach 51:23, 26).

The idea in Proverbs 8, as well as in Sirach 24, is that God created the world through Wisdom, who is personified as standing by his side. The Greek world had a somewhat similar idea, that God created the world through Reason, the Logos, the Word. When John's gospel begins by saying of the Logos, the Word: "He was in the beginning with God. All things came into being through him, and without him not one thing came into being" (1:2-3), the writer is using the Greek philosophical tradition to express the idea of the Jewish wisdom tradition, but he is identifying that Wisdom or Word with Jesus.

So does Matthew do this. Earlier in the chapter Jesus has been speaking of those who criticize his way of life, and he concludes by saying, "Yet wisdom is vindicated by her deeds," in which he is surely referring to himself (11:19). In verses 25-27 of the same chapter he speaks as the bearer of divine wisdom (significantly, nowhere else does the Matthean Jesus sound so much like the Jesus of the Gospel of

John). And here, with our passage, verses 28-30, he issues the dominical invitation, the invitation of Wisdom to come to him and learn.

The heavy burden from which we are promised relief is, against Matthew's background, the burden of the Law. Jewish tradition spoke of the Law as a yoke, but the rabbis spoke of that yoke in the same way that Jesus here speaks of his life: "Whoever takes on the yoke of the Law will be relieved of the yoke of earthly kingdoms and the yoke of worldly care; but whoever throws off the yoke of the Law will be burdened with the yoke of earthly kingdoms and the yoke of worldly care" (Mishnah, Aboth 3:5). This is the yoke Jesus bids us assume, a yoke that will relieve our burdens, the yoke of the Law as Jesus teaches it. "Learn of him" does not mean "learn about him"; it means learn *from* him, and would have been so understood in King James' day. He is the true teacher of Torah, of Wisdom. Since he is identified with God's Word and Wisdom, there is no question of the Law's being abolished. Matthew's Jesus says in the Sermon on the Mount, "Do not think that I have come to abolish the law or the prophets; I have come not to abolish but to fulfill" (5:17).

The teacher who bids us come describes himself as "meek and lowly of heart." He uses here the same word as in Matthew 5:5, where he blesses the meek, "for they will inherit the earth," that is, the land, the long-awaited Kingdom. He knows our burdens for he is one of us, and he summons us to live the life of the Kingdom now, the Kingdom of the Messiah. In putting on the yoke of the Kingdom of God, in living a gentle and humble life like that of our Teacher, our souls find rest.

The yoke he lays on us is easy to bear; the burden we lift is light. Matthew's audience knew that even knowing how to obey all the minute points of the Law was a life's work; actually living by them was impossible. It could easily turn joyous gratitude for the gift of Torah into anxiety and guilt. But Jesus taught that it is really much simpler than this. In answer to the question as to what was the most important commandment in the Law, he responded, "you shall love the Lord your God with all your heart, and with all your soul, and with all your mind, and with all your strength . . ." and "You shall love your neighbor as yourself" (Mark 12:29-31). To the questioner who agreed with him, Jesus said, "You are not far from the Kingdom of God" (Mark 12:34). The story goes that when the great Rabbi Hillel, in the generation before Jesus, was challenged by a brash young man to teach him the whole Law while he stood on one foot, the Rabbi responded, "You will love the Lord your God with all your heart . . . and your neighbor as yourself. That is the whole law and prophets. All the rest is commentary."

When, in the years of the young church's early spread, Gentiles begin coming into the church, there will be a controversy between the conservative faction, who believe that all Christians must observe the entirety of the Mosaic Law, and the liberal party, who believe that there is no such obligation. At a conference called to deal with the issue, the apostle Peter will defend the latter position: "Now therefore why are you putting God to the test by placing on the neck of the disciples a yoke that neither our ancestors nor we have been able to bear? On the contrary, we believe that we will be saved through the grace of the Lord Jesus, just as they will" (Acts 15:10-11).

The easy yoke, the light burden,* is none other than the admonition of the prophet Micah: "He has told you, O mortal, what is good; and what does the LORD require of you, but to do justice, and to love kindness, and to walk humbly with your God?" (Micah 6:8)

~

THE ALTO'S ARIA, "He shall feed his flock like a shepherd," is in the "pastoral key" of F. It is a warm, intimate, enfolding song, with lines descending like the shepherd stooping to pick up a lamb. This is the music of the kind and compassionate Jesus. The soprano's high F modulates into B flat, issuing the dominical invitation to come, to live as disciples of the gentle teacher of divine wisdom. This

---

* "Burthen" is, of course, an archaic form of "burden." It is not spelled that way in Bibles we use today, but the King James Version was revised from time to time after its publication. In these revisions spelling was modernized. The last revision, with which people today are familiar, the "Oxford Standard," was done in 1769. *Messiah* dates from 1741.

melody is built on that of the alto. The prophetic words are elevated to a higher pitch and receive elaboration and fulfillment in the words of the Messiah himself.

There is a textual problem in the score at the soprano's entrance. Usually sung

it is far better to use the variant

After the music of the alto's aria settles to its tonic F, the soprano's "Come" should pierce through and hover momentarily; it is a word to be savored. It is the important word in the text, not the first syllable of the word "un-to" which usually is accented. When sung this way, the soprano's entrance, taking over from the alto an octave higher but in a new key, is one of the sublimest moments in music, and certainly in the oratorio.

Once again the chorus speaks for the people. We assume Messiah's gentle burden and are set free. Here is the rejoicing of a liberated folk. The music is substantial, not ethereal, but it manages to fleet and be wafted as a feather in a breeze.

Part I of the oratorio began with the promise of comfort to God's people. It now ends with the fulfillment of the prophecy. A burdened people have been relieved; a yoke has been lifted from our shoulders — the yoke of our sin and guilt — and another yoke assumed, the yoke of God's grace. The Law is not abrogated; we are not free of demands on us. But we have been set free to live a life of the Kingdom here and now. By our doing so, the burden of earthly kingdoms and worldly care is lifted. The yoke of Messiah's kingdom is a yoke of grace.

# PART II

## 22. CHORUS

**Behold the Lamb of God, that taketh away the sin of the world.** *(John 1:29, slightly modified)*

Moses and Aaron stand before the pharaoh and announce that in the middle of the coming night every firstborn in the land of Egypt will die.

A prophet in exile ponders the mystery of suffering, and sings a song of an innocent one who suffers on behalf of others.

An apocalyptic seer has a vision of the End, with Good at long last victorious over the domain of Evil.

And John the Baptist stands at the water's edge, sees Jesus approaching, and declares of him, "Here is the Lamb of God who takes away the sin of the world!" (John 1:29).

It is appropriate that Part II of *Messiah* begin with John the Baptist, just as did Part I, with the voice crying in the wilderness. We are about to hear of the Messiah's victory, which will entail his death. To bring the Baptist into the picture here seems out of order; he belongs at the beginning of the story. But the librettist takes the liberty of bringing him in a second time. In Part I the Baptist announced the coming of the glory of the Lord in the person of the Messiah; the announcement was taken from the picture of the Baptist in the Synoptic gospels, Matthew, Mark, and Luke. Here the Baptist appears in his Johannine presentation, to announce the saving advent of one who takes away the sin of the world. The words look backward to the Jesus who lifts the burden from the weary and heavy laden, and forward to the passion of the Messiah in the coming sections.

It is John's gospel alone that tells us of this hailing of the Messiah by the Baptist, and it is only in the literature under the name of John that we find the image of Jesus as the Lamb of God. It is a rich motif, with several different roots.

One of these sources is in the tradition of the Passover, the annual Jewish festival celebrating the release of the Hebrews from their bondage in Egypt, an event which may well have taken place

71

in the thirteenth pre-Christian century. In the story in Exodus, Moses and Aaron, his brother and spokesman, present the Egyptian monarch with God's demand that the Israelites be freed. The king refuses, and God strikes Egypt with a plague. This sequence occurs nine times. Each time, after the plague, the pharaoh agrees to freedom for the Hebrews, and then changes his mind. At the end of this series of events, God prepares the final visitation. During the night all the firstborn of Egypt will die. There is not much time; the Hebrews must prepare for a quick departure, and prepare to protect themselves from the death that will scour the countryside that night. A quick meal must be prepared, and it will feature a lamb, specially selected and slaughtered for the occasion. Blood from the animal must be smeared on the doorways of the Hebrew dwellings. Only then will they escape the impending plague.

The event is remembered each spring in Judaism, and its observance had long been known in the time of Jesus. John's gospel interprets Jesus in terms of the Passover lamb. In the other three gospels, the last supper which Jesus eats with his disciple is a Passover meal. In John's gospel it is not. John makes a point that Jesus was on the cross at the time the Passover lambs were slain in preparation for the meal that evening (John 19:14). Though John is the only gospel so to picture Jesus' death, the idea was familiar in early Christianity. Paul declares, "Our paschal (passover) lamb, Christ, has been sacrificed" (I Corinthians 5:7). I Peter 1:19 speaks of our being ransomed from sin by "the precious blood of Christ, like that of a lamb without spot or blemish," such as the Passover lamb was supposed to be. Technically speaking, the Passover lamb was not a sacrifice, since it was not offered on behalf of sin, but by New Testament times the observance had been brought into the whole sacrificial system, with the priesthood officiating at the slaughter. Here, then, is one facet of the picture. Jesus, the good shepherd, is here pictured as a lamb to be sacrificed — not put forward by the people, but by God himself, on our behalf. He is the Lamb of God.

Another strand of thought is in the exilic Isaiah, the prophet with whose words the oratorio opened. In Isaiah 53 there is a long poem picturing a person innocent of misdeed who suffers on behalf of others. The librettist clearly has this passage in mind, for the text of the next four sections of the work will be drawn from it. In that chapter the prophet compares the sufferer to a lamb: "He was oppressed, and he was afflicted, yet he did not open his mouth; like a lamb that is led to the slaughter, and like a sheep that before its shearers is silent, so he did not open his mouth" (Isaiah 53:7). We will have more to say about this passage in the next section.

Yet another motif is woven into the image of the Lamb of God. The precedent for this theme is outside the Scripture, but not outside the traditions with which the scriptural writers were familiar. In the several centuries before Christ, particularly in the second century, there arose among the Jews a genre of literature known as apocalyptic. Like prophecy, it was visionary and concerned itself with the future. But unlike prophecy, it was never oral; it was a written literature from the beginning. Like prophecy, it dealt with the issue of sin and evil, but unlike prophecy, it saw no hope of altering the human situation within the context of history. It saw evil as reaching climactic heights, but expressed the confident hope that God would intervene to override evil in a victory to establish good forever. This faith was expressed in an elaborate symbolism, often bizarre to our minds, involving fantastically constructed animals, significant colors, and numbers that concealed meaning. In the Old Testament the last seven chapters of the book of Daniel are apocalyptic writing. In the New Testament the book of Revelation is the supreme example. These books are so unlike anything else in the Bible that to most modern readers they are unique. But they are not. A great deal of this kind of literature was produced by eschatologically minded Jews in antiquity, and the Christian movement soon took over the genre and used it for its own purposes. A surprising amount of this writing has survived, and it is often quite useful in the interpretation of apocalyptic within the Bible.

A book called the Testament of Joseph, part of a longer work called the Testaments of the Twelve Patriarchs, contains a picture of a lamb who is victorious over a horde of wild animals (19:8). Another reference seems to occur in I Enoch 90:38 (there are problems with

73

the text here), where "the Lord of the sheep" rejoices over a lamb, probably representing the Messiah. In the book of Revelation, the Messiah is pictured as a lamb. The forces of evil "will make war on the Lamb, and the Lamb will conquer them, for he is Lord of lords and King of kings" (17:14). We will return to this particular aspect of the Lamb of God imagery in the great chorus which closes the oratorio.

~

AND SO, as we are about to hear of the Messiah's suffering, the chorus amplifies the salutation of John the Baptist: "Behold the Lamb of God, who takes away the sins of the world!"

This is no joyous chorus. It contrasts sharply with the elation of the preceding section. But it is fitting that the chorus, which sang those happy words of emancipation, be the voice that summons up the prospect of Messiah's passion. We have been liberated, but the liberation was won through the suffering of another. The music is ominous. It is slow, but it should not be too slow. It is easy to let this piece drag. If it does, it can quickly become boring, and it can suggest despair rather than the inexorability of divine determination. This is the force of the line suggesting laboriousness: "that taketh away" — now a pause, almost as if for rest, "the sin of the world," the line rising higher, depicting the heavy weight of sin being lifted from the world by Messiah's agony. The melody shapes itself to the divine task.

### 23. Alto Aria

He was despised and rejected of men, a man of sorrows, and acquainted with grief. *(Isaiah 53:3, modified)*

He gave his back to the smiters, and his cheeks to them that plucked off the hair: he hid not his face from shame and spitting. *(Isaiah 50:6, modified)*

74

## 24. Chorus

Surely he hath borne our griefs and carried our sorrows; he was wounded for our transgressions, he was bruised for our iniquities; the chastisement of our peace was upon him. *(Isaiah 53:4a-5)*

## 25. Chorus

And with his stripes we are healed. *(Isaiah 53:5d)*

## 26. Chorus

All we like sheep have gone astray, we have turned ev'ry one to his own way; and the Lord hath laid on him the iniquity of us all. *(Isaiah 53:6)*

There would have been a full moon that Thursday evening, but they probably took torches with them for light. They wended their way through the city's dark streets after a last meal together, the twelve of them. One of their number had left during supper, but they would see him again before the night was out. Judas' departure had been ominous, and so also were the Teacher's words when he told these disciples that he would not join them at table again until the great messianic banquet: "I will never again drink of this fruit of the vine until that day when I drink it new with you in my Father's kingdom" (Matthew 26:29). In the months to come, in the years to come, they would remember that meal and relive it again and again.

Bravely they sang a hymn before starting out to Gethsemane. On the way, by the torchlight, the one who had earlier stooped to wash the feet of these men told them that all of them would desert him that very night.

We are never specifically told, but this garden, Gethsemane, to which they went was probably on the Mount of Olives, over-looking Jerusalem. It was here a few days earlier that Jesus, at the end of his trek from Galilee, laid eyes on the city spread before him and wept over it (Luke 19:37, 41). It was here, a thousand years or so earlier, that King David, fleeing the city before his rebellious son Absalom, wept (II Samuel 15:30).

Here Jesus offered his agonizing prayer on this his last night. Earlier there had been great throngs. Then there were twelve. Now there were eleven. He takes three of these onto the hillside for prayer. He leaves the three — he leaves them to pray, but they sleep — and he goes on alone to wrestle with his fears and hopes. But the silence is broken by the approaching sound of voices and the rattling of swords. Judas is with these men. He identifies Jesus with a kiss, and the Teacher is rushed brusquely away, deserted now by all his followers, taken to an inquest where he is struck, slapped in the face, and spat upon (Matthew 26:67). "He was despised and rejected by others; a man of suffering, and acquainted with infirmity" (Isaiah 53:3).

During the Advent season, Christians anticipate the celebration of the Messiah's birth with readings from the ancient psalms and prophecies that sang of the king. During Holy Week, Christians enter into the passion of their Lord by recalling the magnificent poem on the Servant of the Lord found among the oracles of the great exilic prophet, in Isaiah 52:13–53:12. No Christian can hear these words without calling to mind Gethsemane, the judgment hall, Golgotha, and the tomb belonging to the wealthy Joseph of Arimathea.

This poem is one of four embedded within Isaiah 40–66 which are collectively known as the Servant Songs, since an unidentified figure called the Servant of the Lord appears in them. The other passages are Isaiah 42:1-4, 49:1-6, and 50:4-9. In the long poem from which these sections of the oratorio take their text, the Servant is one who suffers innocently on behalf of others.

Some scholars believe that these songs — and it is possible that a few other passages could be added to the list — were originally separate from the rest of the book and that they have been worked into the Second Isaiah's work, probably by those who edited the material. The reason for this conjecture is that a Servant of the Lord appears elsewhere in the chapters, but there the Servant is seen as rebellious (48:4), suffering unwillingly (51:21-23), as punishment for his own sins (42:24-25). Other scholars, however, while recognizing that the Suffering Servant passages make up a discrete bit of material, believe that they are indeed an integral part of the composition of this part of the book of Isaiah.

For us this is a minor point. The greatest question raised by these Servant Songs is simply, Who is the Servant? Whom does the prophet have in mind? It is a vexing problem on which Old Testament scholars have no consensus.

At first glance, there seems a simple answer, since in one of the passages, the Servant is specifically identified as Israel: "you are my servant, Israel, in whom I will be glorified" (49:3). Further, the Greek translation of 42:1, though not the Hebrew, makes this identification. It is certainly true that in other sections of the book the Servant is Israel.

The context of Isaiah 41:1 through 42:4 is particularly interesting. The peoples are called on to explain the rise to power of Cyrus of Persia, who defeated Babylon and allowed the exiled peoples to return to their homelands (41:1-4). The peoples have no response; they busy themselves with making idols (41:5-7). Then God speaks to "Israel, my Servant," and promises to uphold and strengthen him (41:8-10). The same sequence occurs later in the passage. God issues a challenge to the nations (41:21-24); there is no response from them (41:25-29); and then the Servant is spoken of, who will bear God's spirit and work for justice on earth (42:1-4; this is the first of the so-called Servant Songs). The one problem with this identification is that in at least one place, 49:5-6, the Servant has a mission *to* Israel.

Could the servant be an individual? Certainly the long poem from which our text is derived sounds biographical, and numerous persons in Israel's history have been suggested as prototypes for the portrait of the Servant. Moses, who led a complaining people across the wilderness to the verge of the Promised Land, which he looked upon but did not live to enter, is a possibility. The prophet may well have in mind Jeremiah, the weeping prophet. Isaiah 49:1, "The LORD called me before I was born, while I was in my mother's womb he named me," sounds very much like the word of the Lord to Jeremiah: "Before I formed you in the womb I knew you, and before you were born I consecrated you; I appointed you a prophet to the nations" (Jeremiah 1:5). The experience of the Servant in chapter 53 is strikingly reminiscent of Jeremiah's sorrows and despair. Perhaps the poem is autobiographical, with the unknown poet pouring out the grief of his own soul.

Given the fluid literary conventions of ancient Israel, it is possible to insist too much on clean answers to the question. It is quite conceivable that the prophet does have in mind one or more of the figures of Israel's past or recent history, but at the same time sees his nation itself as the embodiment of the sorrows and suffering of the past. Perhaps these reflections are the prophet's creative explanation for the exile. Perhaps this is how Israel is to be a light to the nations, through redemptive suffering. Whatever the background, it is a noble vision, and one of the towering heights of biblical literature.

Is the Servant the Messiah? Clearly this is the case in the oratorio and in Christian tradition. Strictly speaking, however, from a literal point of view, these passages are not messianic, since they do not concern the king, the "anointed one." Jewish tradition has never applied the Servant Songs to King Messiah. Indeed, a suffering Messiah is a contradiction in terms; the Messiah's function was to be victorious. The connection of the motif of Messiahship with the motif of the Suffering Servant is Christian in origin, and it may well go back to Jesus himself. When Jesus reads that passage from Isaiah 61:1-2 in the Nazareth synagogue, he may well have been seeing himself as the Servant; the passage does have some similarities to the Servant Songs. As Christians saw it, it was in Jesus' humility and submission that the power of God — redemptive power — was revealed. Paul speaks of receiving a word from God in answer to his prayers: "My grace is sufficient for you, for power is made perfect in weakness" (II Corinthians 12:9). And in Revelation, the symbol chosen for the conquering Christ is not one of the ancient symbols of strength, a lion or a bull, but a lamb (Revelation 17:14), the Lamb of God who takes away the sin of the world.

When Christians read this passage, they read it through a filtering lens, that of their own history, which involves the suffering and death of Jesus. Then they see the images of Jesus and of the Suffering Servant of the Lord converge, and claim that history knows no finer fulfillment of the prophet's vision than that of the Suffering Savior.*

In the oratorio, the alto and the chorus sing these words of the suffering Jesus. "He was despised," perhaps because as the preceding verses states, "he had no form or majesty that we should look at him, nothing in his appearance that we should desire him" (Isaiah 53:2). He was "rejected by others." This is the same verb used by the distraught and desperate Job: "My relatives and my close friends have failed me" (Job 19:14). "A man of sorrows," or more literally, "pains, suffering." "Acquainted with grief," more literally, "sickness." The poet may be working with the image of the quarantined leper.

The libretto breaks the sequence of Isaiah 53 to insert a verse from another of the Servant Songs, Isaiah 50:6. There the servant himself speaks in the first person, describing his determination to bear witness to the word God had given him to reveal to the weary. The experience is clearly reflected in Matthew 26:67: "Then they spat in his face and struck him, and some slapped him." This is the one who had said, "If anyone strikes you on the right cheek, turn the other also" (Matthew 5:39). Isaiah 53:7, part of the passage now being sung, though not included in the text, also depicts the scene: "He was oppressed, and he was afflicted, yet he did not open his mouth; like a lamb that is led to the slaughter, and like a sheep that before its shearers is silent, so he did not open his mouth."

---

* Jews, of course, will read this passage through another lens, that of their own history, and the continued oppression and persecution of Israel throughout the Christian centuries. They will see the Holocaust of the twentieth century, the pogroms of the nineteenth, the persecutions of the eighteenth, the seventeenth, and on back to the exile, where the image of the Servant in exile converges with that of scattered Israel.

When the chorus begins, "Surely he hath borne our griefs," we are standing before the cross. The griefs and sorrows with which the Servant was acquainted were rightfully ours. But he has taken them on himself, suffering them in our stead. "Surely he has borne our infirmities and carried our diseases," reads the New Revised Standard Version, quite legitimately. Matthew, taking a cue from the old Greek translation, which understood the passage in this way, will quote this passage to show how Jesus fulfilled the prophecy in his healing ministry (Matthew 8:17).

All his suffering was due to sin, to "transgressions," to "iniquities." Not his, but ours. "He was wounded for *our* transgressions, crushed for *our* iniquities; upon him was the punishment that made *us* whole," and by his bruises *we* are healed." The awkward phrase "the chastisement of our peace" refers to punishment, a punishment that *he* bore, that has brought us *shalom:* peace, wholeness, all well-being. "Stripes" are brought on by lashes. (Recall Mark 15:15: Pilate, "after flogging Jesus, . . . handed him over to be crucified.") Such stripes are wounds, breaking open the flesh. But in the paradox of this divine suffering, his wounds effect our healing.

The chorus utters its confession: a confession of sin and a confession of faith. "All we like sheep have gone astray, we have all turned to our own way." We are the sheep for whom the Good Shepherd, who carries the lambs in his bosom, may be called on to give his life (John 10:11). "I am the good shepherd. The good shepherd lays down his life for the sheep." This is our confession of sin. "And the Lord has laid on him the iniquity of us all." This is our confession of faith.

Here is the heart of it. As peoples everywhere and always have known, something is amiss with the human race. Things are not as they should be. The intellectual history of humanity knows many explanations — mythological, religious, philosophical. But as the Bible sees it, the primal fault is that we have rebelled against God. The biblical word for this is "sin," and the ancient Israelites read this proclivity in human nature back into creation itself, in the account of Adam and Eve's first act of disobedience. It ruptured the human relationship with God. Humanity's spiritual problem is the restoration of that proper relationship. The primeval history in Genesis teaches that divine punishment does not work; after the flood people were no better off than before. The rift is too broad for leaping. Only God can bridge it. The Bible is not the story of the human quest for God, but of God's seeking us out. He enters into covenant with his people Israel, but though they break the agreement, God persistently remains faithful, through discipline, through grace, through prophetic word, wooing his people back. He does so for no reason other than that he loves us. That is grace. We do not deserve the love or the seeking, but God pursues us.

God does not indulge us. He does not overlook our sin; it must be dealt with. But punishment is not only the only course. Sin may be punished, but this does not restore the relationship. Sin can also be forgiven, and this is the course the God of the Bible sets himself on from the moment God speaks to Abraham in Genesis 12 and bids him begin a journey of faith.

This is what Christian doctrine sees active in the cross of Christ, the very embodiment of costly, forgiving love. Human sin must be dealt with, and on the cross the Word of God made flesh deals with it, by bearing it for us. We can do nothing to save ourselves but to accept this gracious act of God. This acceptance is faith, an abandoning of all attempts to make ourselves right with God through our own resources, an admission of ourselves as sinners, an acceptance of what God has done in Christ for us.

The ancient prophet whose words are here sung spoke directly on the continuum of the biblical story of saving grace.

Herein is gospel, "good tidings of great joy."

~

THE ALTO'S ARIA, "He was despised," asks us to meditate on the cost of our salvation, the divine sorrow. It asks us to watch with the Messiah in the garden. The music is measured and somber; the range of the melody is narrow and concentrated, with frequent long rests between the phrases.

The following rapid succession of three choruses provides a contrast in mood and tempo. Here again the people of God speak. "Surely" is emphatic. "He hath borne our griefs and carried our sorrows" suggests the lifting of weight, much as does the line "that taketh away the sin of the world" in the last chorus, but this time the line emerges from darkness into sunlight. This is the confession of a forgiven people. Then, in "And with his stripes," the composer lingers over the world "healed," as though soothing balm were laid to the wounds.

"All we like sheep" spends most of its length on the wandering of the sheep, the lines suggesting a giddy silliness to our actions. On and on we go astray. But with the shift to adagio at "And the Lord hath laid on him the iniquity of us all," the frantic activity ceases, as we confess in a heavy series of half-notes the seriousness of God's deed in laying the ultimate burden on the innocent and willing one, the Suffering Servant, the Messiah.

"And they crucified him" (Mark 15:24).

## 27. Tenor Recitative

**All they that see him, laugh him to scorn: they shoot out their lips, and shake their heads, saying:** *(Psalm 22:7, modified)*

## 28. Chorus

**He trusted in God that he would deliver him: let him deliver him, if he delight in him.** *(Psalm 22:8, modified)*

The writers of the four gospels knew Scripture well. Often, it would appear, when they wrote of an incident in the life of Jesus, they had some passage in mind, and would write the story in such a way that

82

the attentive reader or listener would hear echoes of the Old Testament.

When Matthew and Mark wrote their accounts of the mocking of Jesus on the cross, they surely had one such passage in mind, and probably two.

The first of these is Psalm 22, verses 7-8 of which are the text of these two sections. The psalm is clearly reflected as Matthew and Mark describe the scene: "Those who passed by derided him, shaking their head, and saying, '. . . If you are the Son of God, come down from the cross" (Matthew 27:39-40). Matthew continues to describe the ironic murmurings of the religious leaders. "He saved others; he cannot save himself. . . . He trusts in God; let God deliver him now, if he wants to" (27:42-43). The words are doubly ironic, for Matthew has quoted Jesus at the scene of his arrest as saying, "Do you think that I cannot appeal to my Father, and he will at once send me more than twelve legions of angels? But how then would the scriptures be fulfilled, which say it must happen in this way?" (26:53-54).

It is a temptation scene, the third and last of the temptations of Jesus. The first is immediately after his baptism, when Satan challenges him to turn stones into bread, and do other things which would gain him a large messianic following. But that is not to be the way of God's anointed one (Matthew 4:1-22; Luke 4:1-13). The second is midway through Jesus' ministry, when he withdraws from the country with his disciples and asks them who they think he is. Peter confesses him — for the first time in Mark's gospel — as the Messiah. It is at this point that Jesus first tells his disciples of his impending suffering, and he does so plainly. Whereupon Peter rebukes Jesus: this cannot be — the Messiah does not suffer. Jesus responds to Peter with the same words which in Matthew he addresses to Satan: "Get behind me, Satan!" (Mark 8:29-33). The way of Messiahship is to be a way of suffering.

Now, on the cross, taunted by those who believe that his dereliction is an obvious sign that he is no Messiah, no Son of God, Jesus keeps his silence. This is the way he has chosen, the way he must go.

Psalm 22, from which Matthew draws in describing the scene

of the jeering, belongs partially to a class of psalms that scholars call laments of an individual (other examples are Psalms 3, 7, 26, and 51). The psalmist bemoans his situation, begging for God's help:

O my God, I cry by day, but you do not answer; and by night, but find no rest. . . . I am a worm, and not human; scorned by others, and despised by the people. . . . Many bulls encircle me . . . they open wide their mouths at me, like a ravening and roaring lion. . . . I am poured out like water and all my bones are out of joint; my heart is like wax; it is melted within my breast. . . . For dogs are all around me; a company of evildoers encircle me. . . . (Psalm 22:2-16)

It is not at all clear from this just what danger the psalmist faced. Was he facing death from disease? Were enemies seeking his life? Was he being persecuted for righteousness' sake? We are not told, and that is just as well. The broad terms and symbols he uses in his plaint allow the reader in any age and place, when faced with threats and despondency, to discover in these words of Scripture an empathetic soul, and phrases to convey his or her own prayer of desperation.

But Psalm 22 is not one of utter despair. The psalmist's prayer is answered. From verse 21b to the end of the song we have an example of the thanksgiving of the individual (again, as scholars call this type):

From the horns of the wild oxen you have rescued me. . . . In the midst of the congregation I will praise you. . . . He did not hide his face from me, but heard when I cried to him. . . . All the ends of the earth shall remember and turn to the LORD. . . . Future generations will be told about the LORD, and proclaim his deliverance to a people yet unborn. (Psalm 22:21b-31).

This makes the Psalm all the more appropriate as a scriptural backdrop for the crucifixion scene, for this suffering and death of the Messiah was to lead to vindication, to resurrection.

The words of our text, as Matthew uses them, are framed by two other references to Psalm 22. In Matthew 27:35, those who had crucified him cast lots over his clothing. The psalmist groans: "They stare and gloat over me; they divide my clothes among themselves, and for my clothing they cast lots" (Psalm 22:17-18).

The other reference is the one that drives home forcefully the point of the psalm, for Matthew and Mark picture Jesus dying with the opening verse of Psalm 22 on his lips: "My God, my God, why have you forsaken me?" To make the words more poignant, both evangelists quote the words in the original — very rare in the gospels — before giving a translation. "Eli, eli, lema sabachthani?" (Matthew 27:46; the slight variation given at Mark 15:34 is explained by the fact that Matthew is giving the quotation in Hebrew, Mark in Aramaic). The onlookers hear the cry to God, "Eli," and think that Jesus is calling on Elijah, another point of irony. We must not miss the real point of despair in the psalmist's complaint. It is not so much that he himself is in danger, but that others are deriding his faith in God. "Commit your cause to the LORD; let him deliver — let him rescue the one in whom he delights" (Psalm 22:8).

A similar irony pervades the scene at the cross. "He trusted in God," the people jeer. Precisely. This is what Jesus had always done. And they cannot see that that is where his trust is even now placed. But the mockers are not trusting; they want proof. "If you are the Son of God, come down from the cross!" (Matthew 27:40). Echoes of Satan in the wilderness: "If you are the Son of God, throw yourself down" (Matthew 4:6). The scoffing crowd did not understand that just at that time when God seemed absent, he was there. But it is only through the eyes of faith that even now can God be present at the cross, or be present in our own afflictions. Our Lord himself was never closer to the will of God than when he cried out, "My God, my God, why have you forsaken me?"

The other passage which the evangelists may well have had in mind when they told the story of the crucifixion is from a book called the Wisdom of Solomon. The name of Solomon has been appropriated. It is a late book, written in Greek, probably in Egypt in the first century before Christ. The Aramaic-speaking Jews of

Palestine would probably have been unfamiliar with it, but Greek-speaking Jews would have known it, since it was part of the Greek Scripture collection which included the Old Testament books, and which is so often quoted in the New Testament. In all probability the gospel writers knew the Wisdom of Solomon. It was always considered Christian Scripture — part of the Old Testament — until the Reformation of the sixteenth century, when the Protestant movement rejected it, along with other books which Protestants relegate to the section called Apocrypha. It did not come to be considered canonical in Judaism, but it remains part of the Bible for the Roman Catholic and the Orthodox churches.

There is an extended passage in chapter 2, placed in the mouth of the ungodly, that is suffused with the imagery of the Suffering Servant and that resonates to the story of Jesus' crucifixion:

"Let us lie in wait for the righteous man,
because he is inconvenient to us and opposes our actions;
he reproaches us for sins against the law,
and accuses us of sins against our training.
He professes to have knowledge of God,
and calls himself a child [or 'servant'] of the Lord.
He became to us a reproof of our thoughts;
the very sight of him is a burden to us,
because his manner of life is unlike that of others,
and his ways are strange.
We are considered by him as something base,
and he avoids our ways as unclean;
he calls the last end of the righteous happy,
and boasts that God is his father.
Let us see if his words are true,
and let us test what will happen at the end of his life;
for if the righteous man is God's child ['son'],
he will help him,
and will deliver him from the hand of his adversaries.
Let us test him with insult and torture,
so that we may find out how gentle he is,

and make trial of his forbearance.
Let us condemn him to a shameful death,
for, according to what he says, he will be protected."
Thus they reasoned, but they were led astray,
for their wickedness blinded them,
and they did not know the secret purposes of God. . . .

(Wisdom 2:12-22)

~

The tenor's short recitative, to a frenzied accompaniment, is hostile, shrill, and jeering. The chorus sings the taunting. When the second syllable of "de*liv*er," on the beat, goes up an interval of a third with the last syllable coming down a fourth, it has the effect of a punch in the belly. The runs on the word "de*light*" have an ironic quality. The word sounds like jeering laughter, but it can also be heard as God's exultant pleasure in the one to whom he spoke at Jesus' baptism: "You are my Son, the Beloved; with you I am well pleased" (Mark 1:11). A further irony is that this is the Expected One, "the messenger of the covenant, whom ye delight in," as the bass has sung earlier.

Up to this point, the chorus has been the people of God, capping off prophetic words or making confession. But here it is the unruly crowd having their obscene fun at a public execution. Yet in a deeper sense it is the same chorus, the chorus of those for whom Jesus dies. It is the voice of unfaith within us all, even within the people of God. Luke's Jesus does not utter the cry of abandonment from the cross. Instead he prays, "Father, forgive them; for they do not know what they are doing" (Luke 23:34).

### 29. TENOR RECITATIVE

**Thy rebuke hath broken his heart; he is full of heaviness. He looked for some to have pity on him, but there was no man, neither found he any to comfort him.** *(Psalm 69:20, much modified)*

**Behold, and see if there be any sorrow like unto his sorrow!** *(Lamentations 1:12, modified)*

For the recitative, the librettist has once again turned to the Psalter, to another lament of the individual, Psalm 69. And once more, it is a psalm whose words are reflected in the gospel account of the crucifixion. No more than with Psalm 22 can we be certain of the woes actually befalling the psalmist, though verse 33 may indicate that he was imprisoned.

The entirety of this psalm can hardly be taken as a meditation on the passion of Jesus. This poet confesses his sin (69:5), and breaks out in a vindictive string of curses against his enemies (69:22-29). Still Psalm 69 is referred to more often in the New Testament than any other except Psalm 22, and the church has long read it messianically. When the Gospel of John describes Jesus' cleaning of the Temple, he has the disciples think of verse 9: "It is zeal for your house that has consumed me" (John 2:17). Paul will quote the second half of that same verse in Romans 15:3 and apply it to Christ: "The insults of those who insult you have fallen on me."

The psalm begins with the same Job-like motif as the opening of Psalm 22: "Save me, O God, for the waters have come up to my neck. . . . My eyes grow dim with waiting for my God" (Psalm 69:1-3). The following stanzas bemoan the poet's humiliation and reproach, and express confidence that the steadfast love of the Lord will ultimately vindicate him. Like Psalm 22, the concluding stanza is a psalm of praise to the God who hears the prayers of the oppressed.

It is in verse 20 that we find our text, much modified from the biblical context, where the complaint is in the first person: "I looked for pity, but there was none, and for comforters, but I found none."

This is not literally true of the crucifixion scene. According to the gospel accounts, several of his relatives and friends attended him. His mother Mary was there (John 19:25), as were his mother's sister

Mary (John 19:25), yet another Mary, the mother of two men who must have been known to the early tradition, James and Moses (Matthew 27:56; Mark 15:40 — possibly the same as Jesus' aunt Mary), Mary Magdalene, that figure whom tradition has so besmirched — there is no indication that she was a prostitute (Matthew 27:56; Mark 15:40; John 19:25). Also present were Salome, Joanna, and Susanna, three of the women who traveled with Jesus and the Twelve in Galilee during his ministry, as well as other women (Mark 15:40-41; Luke 23:49; Luke 8:2-3). The mother of the disciples James and John was there (Matthew 27:56). Luke also includes "all his acquaintances" (23:49), but is not specific about who he means; he most pointedly does not hint that any of the disciples were there.

Besides the soldiers, the only male figure mentioned at the cross is the mysterious person known as the "beloved disciple" or "the other disciple," who appears numerous times in the Gospel of John. Tradition, though not the gospel itself, identifies this man with John the disciple and reputed author of the book. He may well have been Lazarus of Bethany, whom Jesus raised from the dead and is the only figure in the book of whom it is specifically said, "he loved him" (John 11:36). According to Matthew, Mark, and Luke, all this group were standing off at some distance, but the group whom John names are described as being there at the cross, for Jesus directly addresses his mother and the beloved disciple (John 19:26-27).

The four gospels differ somewhat in the specific persons involved, but all four make it clear that it is these women who attended Jesus at his death and burial (Joseph of Arimathea is mentioned in connection with the burial arrangements, but none of the disciples is present). Women were also the first at the empty tomb, the first to give witness to the resurrection.

So there were people around Jesus when he died, women who knew and loved him, but also those of whom the psalmist said, "More in number than the hairs of my head are those who hate me without cause; many are those who would destroy me, my enemies who accuse me falsely" (Psalm 69:4). Jesus had quoted this verse to his disciples in his farewell speech to his disciples (John 15:25).

It is verse 21 in the psalm, the one following our text, that ties down the relevance of this psalm for the crucifixion scene: "They gave me poison for food, and for my thirst they gave me vinegar to drink." All four of the gospels refer, at least obliquely, to these lines in their accounts of events at the cross, though they treat them somewhat differently.

Mark and Matthew describe two separate scenes in which Jesus is offered drink. As Mark tells it, before Jesus is crucified, he is offered a potion of wine and myrrh, apparently as a narcotic or pain reliever. (The Talmud tells us that certain Jewish women in Jerusalem took it on themselves to offer pain relievers to those about to be executed, following the prescription of Proverbs 31:6. Mark implies, however, that it is the executioners who make the offer.) Jesus refuses the drink, consistent with Mark's theme that the way of suffering is the way that Jesus chose, and he will not dull that suffering at the climactic point. As Matthew tells it, before Jesus is crucified he is offered a mixture of wine and gall, which Jesus tastes, but then refuses. This is consistent with Matthew's presentation of Jesus' experience fulfilling Scripture. Psalm 69:21 — "They gave me poison [gall] for food" — is reflected here. The offer is not an act of mercy but of cruelty, and Jesus rejects it.

At the point when Jesus is about to expire, and he shouts the cry of dereliction, and people think he is calling on Elijah, Mark has one of the bystanders put vinegar on a sponge stuck on a reed (presumably to lift it to Jesus' mouth) and offer it to him to drink. The liquid is probably actually a sour wine that was consumed by the common soldiers. The person does this apparently to revive him, because he wants to see, mockingly, if Elijah really is going to rescue him (Mark 15:34-36). But as Matthew tells it, the bystanders try to stop the man from offering the drink, apparently because it might revive him and they want to see, mockingly, if Elijah is going to appear (Matthew 27:46-49). Luke simply says that soldiers mocked him and offered him vinegar (Luke 23:36).

We are led to assume that Jesus accepted the vinegary wine. Only John specifically says so, but John uses the scene to a different effect. There, Jesus realizes that he is on the verge of death, and

90

mutters, "I am thirsty." Someone then puts a sponge of vinegar on hyssop, puts it to Jesus' mouth, and he accepts it. This is the climactic scene for John's gospel. Unlike Matthew and Mark, John speaks of the sponge as being put on hyssop rather than a reed. This is a strange picture; hyssop is an herb. One could hardly stick it into a sponge and use it to lift the sponge. Possibly there is a textual error. The Greek word for "javelin" is very similar to the word "hyssop," and conceivably the two words could have been confused. There is some small degree of manuscript evidence for this — very small — but all critical logic is against the conjecture. Hyssop, however, has tie-ins with the Passover ritual, and John is picturing Jesus as the Paschal Lamb, dying at the time that the lambs for the Passover meal that evening were being slaughtered (John 19:14). Hyssop is consistent with John's theme. And there may be more realism to the picture than we think. Given what we have come to know in recent years about the gruesomeness of crucifixions (one's feet had to be only just off the ground, and the body was often contorted), Jesus' head may well have been lower than those of the onlookers, and the vinegar could have been offered on a sprig of hyssop.

John's point, however, is that this is the one who had turned water into wine, a miracle reported only in John (2:1-11). This is the one who told the woman at the well in Samaria, "Those who drink of the water that I will give them will never be thirsty. The water that I will give will become in them a spring of water gushing up to eternal life" (John 4:14). The evangelist John's acute sense of irony is never more evident than when the one who offers humanity the water of life dies in thirst, with the sour taste of vinegar on his tongue.

Such was the pity shown him. Such was his dying comfort.

Hard on this desolate plaint comes the aria, with the theme of abandonment carried through with a verse from Lamentations, 1:12. The short book of Lamentations is a series of five dirges over the city of Jerusalem after its fall to Babylonia in 587 B.C. It was written at that time or shortly thereafter. Tradition, though not the text, has ascribed it to Jeremiah, although internal evidence would indicate that he is not the author, as similar as the theme of the book is to some of the motifs in Jeremiah's prophecy.

Chapter 1 bemoans the desolation of the destroyed city, pictured as a widow, a princess fallen from power, a mother bereft of her children. She confesses her sins, acknowledges the justice of God's punishment, and offers herself as an advertisement to the nations of the world of the implications of the divine righteousness. In such a vein, she speaks to those who know of her fate, who walk the deserted streets: "Is it nothing to you, all you who pass by? Look and see if there is any sorrow like my sorrow, which was brought upon me, which the LORD has inflicted on the day of his fierce anger" (1:12).

Jerusalem is suffering for her own sins, and the Servant is suffering for the sins of others, but there is common ground in the theme of desolation, abandonment, and the appeal to witness the gravity of God's judgment, and God's sacrificial love.

~

BOTH THE recitative and the aria are plaintive, desirous against any hope of offering pity and comfort to the one who found none, willing to sympathize with a grief and sorrow too profound for sympathy, to which the proper response can be only solemn awe in the presence of the one "who, though he was in the form of God . . . emptied himself, taking the form of a slave. . . . And being found in human form, he humbled himself and became obedient to the point of death — even death on a cross" (Philippians 2:6-8).

## 31. TENOR RECITATIVE

**He was cut off out of the land of the living; for the transgression of thy people was he stricken.** *(Isaiah 53:8, modified)*

## 32. TENOR ARIA

**But thou didst not leave his soul in hell; nor didst thou suffer thy Holy One to see corruption.** *(Psalm 16:10, modified)*

And so Jesus breathed his last. To tell us so, the libretto once again turns to the Song of the Suffering Servant in Isaiah 53, to the sequence of verses we heard earlier, from "He was despised" through "All we like sheep." Here the death of the servant is spoken of:

> By a perversion of justice he was taken away.
>> Who could have imagined his future?
> For he was cut off from the land of the living,
>> stricken for the transgression of my people.
> They made his grave with the wicked
>> and his tomb with the rich,
> although he had done no violence,
>> and there was no deceit in his mouth.
>
> (Isaiah 53:8-9)

The gospels say nothing about Jesus' being buried along with the wicked, although we are told that he was buried in the private tomb of an influential sympathizer, Joseph of Arimathea, who was presumably rich.

But "who could have imagined his future?" He was to rise from the dead, and with his resurrection the Christian movement began. Some early Christians must have asked themselves a question: Where was Jesus from the time of his death until his resurrection? If he was dead, as surely he was, he must have gone to the land of the dead. As early as I Peter we find speculation about this: "He went and made a proclamation to the spirits in prison" (3:19, referring specifically to people from Noah's time); and "The gospel was proclaimed even to the dead, so that, although they had been judged in the flesh as everyone is judged, they might live in the Spirit as God does" (4:6).

It is not at all certain what the author of this book is speaking of. One suggestion is that the reference originally was to the ancient Enoch, not to Christ at all. There is an ancient Jewish tradition that Enoch did indeed preach to imprisoned angels, and an interesting case can be made for the possibility that the name Enoch was mistakenly omitted from I Peter 3:19 by some early scribe. There is no manuscript evidence to support this, however, and it must remain purely speculative.

The idea did develop, at any rate, that Christ, after dying on the cross, went to hell to preach the gospel there. This idea, of the Descent into Hell, or the Harrowing of Hell, is one with which Christian doctrine has never been entirely comfortable. It is reflected in the Apostles' Creed, which contains the line "he descended into hell," a clause that many congregations see fit to omit in the recitation.

The libretto of *Messiah* apparently has this idea in mind for the tenor's aria, "But thou didst not leave his soul in hell," the text of which is a modification of Psalm 16:10. It is a joyous psalm, full of gratitude for the Lord's having granted the psalmist a good life, and full of faith that the Lord will protect him from death. The relevant words are: "Therefore my heart is glad, and my soul [literally, "my glory"] rejoices; my body also rests secure. For you do not give me up to Sheol, or let your faithful one see the Pit" (Psalm 16:9-10).

To place these words in their context, we must first realize that the modern Western view of human existence is not the same as that of the Old Testament. The Old Testament writings do not conceive of a meaningful life after death. We find there no Heaven or Hell in the later Jewish or in the Christian sense. Hebrew has no word for Heaven, as the domain of God, other than the simple word for "sky." Nor is there a word for Hell; there was no such word because there was no such concept. When a person died, it was believed that he or she went to Sheol, the land of the dead, often mistakenly translated "hell" in the King James Version. Sheol was not conceived as a compartmentalized place of blessing or punishment. It was where dead people went, and if one could speak of life there at all, it was only in a shady, shadowy way, not far from the Greek idea of Hades.

One of the psalmists, facing death, described that realm as follows: "For my soul is full of troubles, and my life draws near to Sheol. I am counted among those who go down to the Pit; I am like those who have no help, like those forsaken among the dead, like the slain that lie in the grave, like those whom you remember no more, for they are cut off from your hand" (Psalm 88:3-5). "Do you work wonders for the dead? Do the shades rise up to praise you? Is your steadfast love declared in the grave, or your faithfulness in Abaddon? Are your wonders known in the darkness, or your saving help in the land of forgetfulness?" (Psalm 88:10-12). So also Psalm 115:16-17: "The heavens are the LORD's heavens, but the earth he has given to human beings. The dead do not praise the LORD, nor do any that go down into silence."

The despairing Job, on the other hand, yearns for death: "There the wicked cease from troubling, and there the weary are at rest. There the prisoners are at ease together; they do not hear the voice of the taskmaster. The small and the great are there, and the slaves are free from their masters" (Job 3:17-19). Sheol is thought of as in the depths; some passages picture God as present there, and others see him as absent. "For in death there is no remembrance of you; in Sheol who can give you praise?" (Psalm 6:5). But "Where can I go from your spirit? Or where can I flee from your presence? If I ascend to heaven, you are there; if I make my bed in Sheol, you are there" (Psalm 139:8).

Rescue from Sheol thus becomes a figure for rescue from death. "O LORD my God, I cried to you for help, and you have healed me. O LORD, you brought up my soul from Sheol, restored me to life from among those gone down to the Pit" (Psalm 30:3). Sheol, its synonym Abaddon, as well as the Pit, the grave — all are used in the Old Testament as figures for death.

The orthodox belief was that if God were to reward the righteous and punish the wicked, it must be done in this life. After death it would be too late. Job, in profoundest agony although innocent of sin, protests his innocence to his three comforters and to God. In that book, the problem of innocent suffering is wrestled with at great length and in the grandest poetry of the Bible, but nowhere does Job, the three friends, the young Elihu, or even God suggest that the answer may lie beyond the grave, that the righteous may receive their reward and the wicked their punishment in a hereafter (unless Job 19:25 is such an insight, but more about that later).

One of the changes that came about in the Old Testament religion as a result of the exile was the development in the belief in a meaningful life after death. Perhaps this was due to further inspired reflection on the problem of suffering. Perhaps it was the insight gained from exposure to Persian religion. Perhaps it was both; it would not have been the first time that Israelite religion emerged from a crisis of faith with greater profundity. In the very latest strata of the Old Testament, this new idea begins to be evident.

The only unmistakable reference to the future life in the Old Testament is in Daniel, a book from the second century B.C.: "many of those who sleep in the dust of the earth shall awake, some to everlasting life, and some to shame and everlasting contempt" (Daniel 12:9). Possibly from the third century come the chapters in Isaiah 24–26 called the Isaiah Apocalypse, three chapters which hang together but appear to be of much later date than the surrounding material. In this passage we find Isaiah 26:19: "Your dead shall live, their corpses shall rise." This may well be, like Ezekiel's vision of the valley of dry bones in Ezekiel 37, a reference to the renewal of the nation, but it may possibly refer to the resurrection of the individual.

Not all Jews accepted this new idea. The conservative Sadducees, the priestly party of New Testament times, ridiculed the notion of a life after death. Even the book of Ecclesiastes, accepted by all as Holy Scripture, is skeptical. "The fate of humans and the fate of animals is the same; as one dies, so dies the other. They all have the same breath, and humans have no advantage over the animals; for all is vanity. All go to one place; all are from the dust, and all turn to dust again. Who knows whether the human spirit goes upward and the spirit of animals goes downward to the earth?"

(Ecclesiastes 3:19-21). This book, certainly not from the hand of the traditional author, Solomon, is also of late date, possibly as late as the third century B.C.

Psalm 16, from which our text is taken, cannot be securely dated. The natural interpretation of its language is that the poet is thanking God for saving him from death: "You do not give me up to Sheol, or let your faithful one see the Pit." It is not inconceivable, however, that this is a late psalm, and resurrection is intended.

By the time of the New Testament, the doctrine of a life after death, of Heaven and Hell, was well established in most circles of Judaism, and this allowed a fresh reading and richer interpretation of many of the old Scriptures that dealt with Sheol. What was once written praising God for rescuing one from the brink of death now could be seen as praise for salvation from everlasting death. God's beneficent will and life-giving power is the continuum of this line of reinterpretation.

Handel has used this verse from Psalm 16 to refer to Jesus' escape from death, perhaps with reference to the visitation of Hell, but the same verse is used in the New Testament of Jesus' resurrection. Peter quotes it in his Pentecost sermon in Acts 2:27.

~

THE BRIEF RECITATIVE representing Jesus' death is sung to only a few accompanying chords. The melody is in a surprisingly high range for a somber text, suggesting perhaps that a superhuman business is being conducted. The final two notes, "stricken," seem to strike the death blow, descending from E to B. From the dark B minor of the recitative we move into the bright key of A for the aria, the tenor's announcement to us that death has not had the final word, publishing the good tidings to all before the magnificent chorus of the resurrection that follows.

# 33. CHORUS

Lift up your heads, O ye gates, and be ye lift up, ye
everlasting doors, and the King of Glory shall come in!
Who is this King of Glory? The Lord strong and mighty,
the Lord mighty in battle. Lift up your heads, O ye
gates, and be ye lift up, ye everlasting doors, and the
King of Glory shall come in! Who is the King of Glory?
The Lord of Hosts, he is the King of Glory. *(Psalm
24:7-10, modified)*

The long summer drought is over. The heat has begun to moderate,
and perhaps the first of the welcome autumn rains have already
fallen on the dry countryside. A new year is beginning in Israel, and
pilgrims from across the land are flocking to the Holy City for the
annual celebration.

Crowds mill and murmur outside one of the city gates, surrounding a band of priests. The center of everyone's attention is the
Ark of the Covenant, the holiest object in Israel, which some of the
priests are supporting on long poles thrust through rings mounted
on the sides of the chest. They dare not touch it, for it is holy, and
they would die from contact with it.

A ritual is about to be reenacted, one which will confess the
Lord as the God of creation, who brings about the renewal of the
earth with the return of the rainfall; one in which the people will
reaffirm the ancient covenant enacted with their God on Mount
Sinai; one in which God's pleasure in establishing the line of David
the Anointed One on the throne of Israel will be celebrated.

The Ark of the Covenant is at the center of the themes. It was
the throne of God himself, who was conceived as seated invisibly
on it, "enthroned above the cherubim" (II Kings 19:15) that were
fashioned of gold on either side of the lid of the ark, known as the
mercy seat. The chest itself contained the tables of the Ten Commandments, the heart of the covenant.

In the old days of settlement in the land, the priests would
take the ark into battle when the Israelites did battle with the

Philistines, to signify God's presence. It had once even been captured by the enemy, but when plagues broke out among them they were all too happy to return it (I Samuel 6–7). In those days it was kept at the village of Shiloh, where the Tabernacle, the mobile collapsible place of worship that served the people during their wilderness wanderings, had found a home.

When David, as warrior king, completed the conquest of Canaan by capturing the stronghold of Jerusalem, he demonstrated his genius by having the apparatus of worship, ark and Tabernacle, transported to the city which now became his capital. Jerusalem, David's city, became the focus of the political and the religious loyalties of the nation, enhancing David's hold on power and underscoring the sanctity of the eternal Davidic kingship.

The occasion of the ark's arrival in Jerusalem is about to be reenacted, and the people raise a psalm in honor of the Lord of creation:

> The earth is the LORD's and all that is in it,
>     the world, and those who live in it;
> for he has founded on the seas,
>     and established it on the rivers.
>
> (Psalm 24:1-2)

Antiphonal singing begins, as those outside the gates raise the question:

> "Who shall ascend the hill of the LORD?
>     And who shall stand in his holy place?"
>
> (Psalm 24:3)

Priests inside the city gates chant the response:

> "Those who have clean hands and pure hearts,
>     who do not lift up their souls to what is false,
>     and do not swear deceitfully.
> They will receive blessing from the LORD

and vindication from the God of their salvation.
    Such is the company of those who seek him,
        who seek the face of the God of Jacob."

(Psalm 24:4-6)

Now the procession is ready to enter, carrying the ark back to its place in the Holy of Holies in the Temple. Those outside sing out:

"Lift up your heads, O gates!
    and be lifted up, O ancient doors!
    that the King of glory may come in."

(Psalm 24:7)

Again, the chorus from inside the gates:

"Who is the King of glory?"

The response from outside:

"The LORD, strong and mighty,
the LORD, mighty in battle.
Lift up your heads, O gates!
and be lifted up, O ancient doors!
that the King of glory may come in."

(Psalm 24:8-9)

Once more, from those who guard the gates, asking as it were for proper identification, for the password:

"Who is this King of glory?"

And the triumphant response,

"The LORD of hosts,
he is the King of glory."

(Psalm 24:10)

The gates swing open, and a joyful people proceed through the gateway and up to the Temple mount, perhaps singing Psalm 47: "God has gone up with a shout, the LORD with the sound of a trumpet" (Psalm 47:5).

The ceremony described here is a speculative reconstruction. Such an event is nowhere described in the Bible in so many words, but scholars have posited it from various hints in the historical books of a ceremony of covenant renewal, and from the content of some of the psalms. Psalms 15 and 47 are others which may have been used on such occasions. Not all scholars agree that such a New Year's festival in the fall of the year even existed, but for many, it is a reasonable supposition, and explains a number of things.

Regardless of its historical setting, the words of Psalm 24, loosed from calendrical and geographical mooring, have been used by Handel's librettist as an entrance liturgy of a different nature. It hymns the resurrection of the Messiah, the Anointed One.

A characteristic of poetry is that its meaning does not reside in the simple semantic content of the words. The reader must see the image that the words project, fuller and richer than a mere grammatical analysis of the poem would suggest. Part of the poetry of the oratorio's structure is that, with the sole exception of the shepherds in the fields, the story we are hearing is not depicted by the words but only suggested by them. The skill of the librettist is nowhere better seen than in the choice of this psalm to suggest the Lord's resurrection. The New Testament itself does not actually depict the resurrection. There are accounts of the discovery of the empty tomb, and there are narratives in which the risen Jesus appears to his disciples and other believers, but the passage from death to life is left as an undescribed mystery.

～

THIS IS A triumphant chorus, hymning the return of the glorious King, the Lord mighty in battle, from his victory over death and the grave, and his entry into his own place. There is powerful contrast in the picture of massive stone lintels giving way before the cosmic king. One remembers Solomon's prayer at the dedication of the Temple: "But will God indeed dwell on the earth? Even heaven and earth cannot contain you, much less this house that I have built" (I Kings 8:27).

## 34. Tenor Recitative

**Unto which of the angels said he at any time: thou art my son, this day have I begotten thee?** *(Hebrews 1:5a, modified)*

## 35. Chorus

**Let all the angels of God worship him.** *(Hebrews 1:6b)*

The academician of the New Testament is the anonymous author of the Letter to the Hebrews. In this book a careful logic is being pursued, a logic based on a particular strain of ancient Greek philosophy which is more alien to most readers of the Bible than is the Old Testament, with which the author of Hebrews is also intimately familiar.

The philosophy is that of Plato. If our author was not a student of Plato's writings firsthand, he was almost certainly familiar with the Jewish philosopher Philo, of the early first century of the Christian era. Philo had undertaken to interpret Judaism and the Jewish Scriptures in terms of Plato's philosophy. This is what the author to the Hebrews is doing as well, but he is using his platonized interpretation to point to Jesus Christ as the fulfillment of Scripture.

Plato believed that this world and the things of this world are not fundamentally real. What we experience about us are only copies, shadows, reflections of a real order of existence which is a heavenly one. The author to the Hebrews places this idea at the service of the gospel. The earthly Temple with its priesthood and sacrificial system is simply a copy of the heavenly Temple, where

Jesus Christ ministers as the true High Priest, having given himself as the ultimate sacrifice (Hebrews 8:1-6; 10:1-4, 12-14).

The writer begins the book with a long, elaborate, rolling, alliterative sentence in which he states that God, in these latter days, has spoken to humanity definitively through his Son. At the end of the sentence he declares that the Son is superior to the angels, just as his name is superior to theirs (1:1-4).

It is at this point that our text begins. In the recitative we have a quotation from a New Testament writer quoting a psalm. It is Psalm 2, one of the royal, or messianic, psalms. It is widely thought that early Christians used collections of scriptural quotations which they applied to Christ. Perhaps our writer is using such a "testimony book" as a source for this and his many other quotations from the Old Testament. At any rate, it is clear that by the time of this writing — late first century — the royal psalms were being used by Christians as references to Jesus the Messiah. Our writer, clearly writing to other Christians, simply assumes this. He does not argue the point, as he might were he writing for a Jewish audience that needed to be convinced. With an audience sympathetic to his presuppositions, the writer proceeds with his argument.

The second psalm may well have been composed for the enthronement of a king. We will hear more words from this psalm in Section 40-43, but our attention is now on verse 7, in which God speaks to the new king: "You are my son; today I have begotten you." Here we must remember the terms of the covenant with David in II Samuel 7, whereby God speaks of Solomon, who will succeed David on the throne, as his own son (II Samuel 7:14).

Christ is unique, says our author. God was in the psalm speaking of the Messiah as his Son, and he never spoke to any angel in such a fashion. Therefore Jesus is superior to the angels. (It is possible, though not at all a necessary assumption, that the audience for Hebrews was much involved with speculation about hierarchies of angels, so that our writer's point in 1:4 was something that needed to be proven.)

Hebrews 1:5 is not the only place in the New Testament where this verse from the Psalms is quoted. In Acts 13:33, Paul quotes it in the context of a sermon he delivers on one of his missionary journeys. There the application is made to the resurrection and exaltation of Jesus. Comparable to the ancient king's enthronement, Jesus' resurrection is the occasion on which his divine sonship begins. Paul says as much in his own words in Romans 1:1-4: Jesus was "declared to be Son of God with power according to the spirit of holiness by resurrection from the dead. . . ."

This appears to be the earliest Christian answer to the question, "When did Jesus become Son of God?" But it is not the only answer. Paul's view is the first we have; of the writings in the New Testament, Paul's are the earliest. By the time we come to the Gospel of Mark, probably the first of the gospels, we have a voice from heaven after Jesus' baptism, speaking to him alone: "You are my Son, the Beloved" (Mark 1:11). Here God seems to reveal the divine sonship to Jesus at the baptism. Matthew and Luke also record this, though in Matthew the voice speaks of Jesus in the third person, as though to an audience. In each of these three gospels are textual variants, with many manuscripts adding the words of Psalm 2:7, "today I have begotten you." The noncanonical Gospel of the Ebionites says the same. The reference to the psalm is not a genuine text in any of the canonical gospels, but it does witness to the strength of the belief among some early Christians that Jesus was "adopted" Son of God on the occasion of his baptism.

By the time Matthew and Luke are written, Jesus' office as Son of God is established at his birth. These two gospels are the sources of the accounts of the virginal conception. Finally, by the end of the first century and the Gospel of John, the divine sonship is read back into eternity before all time and creation (John 1). As Christians reflected on the magnitude of the claim that Jesus was the Messiah, the Son of God, their thinkers expressed that belief in different ways, by seizing on different aspects of the story of Jesus as opportunities for making the point.

It is in the context of the exaltation of Jesus that Hebrews cites the verse from Psalm 2, and this is its use in the oratorio, following as it does immediately on the Resurrection chorus, "Lift Up Your Heads."

As the author's argument progresses he moves on to say that the Son is worshiped by the angels — the text of the aria.

This is a problematic passage. The author is quoting something, but it is not perfectly clear just what. This line does not appear in the text of the traditional Hebrew Bible, but something close to it is found in the ancient Greek translation, at Deuteronomy 32:43: "Let all the sons of God worship him. . . . let all the angels of God ascribe to him strength" (the reference is to their worshiping God). The first of these two lines is found in the Dead Sea Scrolls, and the New Revised Standard Version translates it as part of the Deuteronomy text. The author of Hebrews is either conflating two lines of the Greek Deuteronomy, or has a conflated text before him. On the other hand, it is possible that he is referring to the old Greek translation of Psalm 97:7, which contains the line "Worship him, all his angels." The Hebrew of that line reads, "All gods bow down before him."

The point in the oratorio, however, is clear. After the King has entered, he is worshiped by the host of heaven. The chorus is exultant.

## 36. Bass Aria

**Thou art gone up on high, thou hast led captivity captive, and received gifts for men, yea, even for thine enemies, that the Lord God might dwell among them.**
*(Psalm 68:18, much modified)*

Luke is the only one of the four evangelists who tells us of the ascension of Jesus into heaven, but he tells it twice. At the very end of his gospel, he tells us that the risen Jesus, whose appearances have been related in the last chapter, blessed his disciples and was carried up into heaven (Luke 24:51). Luke expands on this scene at the beginning of the book of Acts. The same author is responsible for both books; the Gospel of Luke is volume one, the book of Acts volume two of a history of the work of Jesus.

In Acts 1, we are told that after the resurrection of Jesus from the dead, he appeared to his followers from time to time over a forty-day period. In his final scene with them, the disciples ask if he is now going to restore the Davidic kingdom. Jesus deflects the question. He tells them that the Father alone knows when that will be, that it is not for them to know. But he promises them that the Holy Spirit will come on them, and that they will be his witnesses from Jerusalem to the ends of the earth. Then as they watched, he rose into the air until he was hidden by the clouds (Acts 1:6-9). This is the scene known as the Ascension of Christ, and it is this that the bass sings of in the aria drawn from Psalm 68:18.

The person who consults this verse in the King James Version will discover some startling differences between it and Handel's text, although the meaning is substantially the same. Part of the explanation for this is that while the librettist used the King James Version as his base, though taking small liberties with it on occasion, for quotations from the Psalms he used the version found in the Book of Common Prayer. This version of the Psalms is that of the Great Bible of 1539, seventy-two years older than the King James translation. The acceptance of the King James Version after it appeared in 1611 was quite slow. Not until 1662 were its readings incorporated into the Book of Common Prayer, the liturgical book of the Church of England; but even then, for the Psalter, the older version was retained. Of all parts of the Bible, the Psalms would be the most familiar to the faithful of the Church of England, and there may well have been concern that hearing the Psalms in a new form (the King James) would be unsettling. Only with revisions of the Prayer Book in recent years has the Great Bible Psalter been replaced, but with more recent translations than that of 1611. When the *Oxford Dictionary of Quotations* cites biblical passages, they are always from the King James Version, except for quotations from the Psalms. These are quoted from the Book of Common Prayer, that form being more familiar to the Anglican public.

But this is only part of the explanation for the difference between our oratorio text and that of the King James. The fact is that Psalm 68 is the most challenging psalm in the Psalter for the translator and interpreter. Its Hebrew is difficult and it seems to lack coherence. So problematic is it for scholars that the suggestion has been made that Psalm 68 is not even a psalm, but an index of first lines to a collection of psalms now lost. One need only glance at the wide variations among modern translations of this verse to appreciate the difficulty of consensus. There is a significant difference between the Revised Standard Version of 1952 and the New Revised Standard Version of 1990. The difference is even more startling between the New English Bible of 1970 and its revision, the Revised English Bible.

It is probably best to view this psalm as another of the entrance liturgy psalms, such as Psalm 24, discussed earlier in Section 33, Lift Up Your Heads. Here, however, the emphasis is on the Lord as divine warrior, returning home victorious in battle. There are military motifs, as in: "Let God rise up, let his enemies be scattered" (v. 1); "The women at home divide the spoil . . ." (v. 12).

There is also the theme of creation, as a theophany is described: "O God, when you went out before your people . . . the earth quaked, the heavens poured down rain. . . . Rain in abundance, O God, you showered abroad; you restored your heritage when it languished . . ." (vv. 7-9). This does sound remarkably appropriate for a fall festival at the beginning of the new year's first rains.

Also in this psalm, and we have it in the bass aria, is the motif of God returning to his place in the Temple. "The Lord came from Sinai into the holy place" (v. 7). "Thou hast gone up on high" surely refers in the context to God's going to the Temple Mount: "You ascended the high mount" (v. 18). "Awesome is God in his sanctuary, the God of Israel; he gives power and strength to his people. Blessed be God!" (v. 35).

We even have in this psalm a description of the liturgical procession: "Your solemn processions are seen, O God, the processions of my God, my King, into the sanctuary — the singers in front, the musicians last, between them girls playing tambourines" (vv. 24-25).

If the line "Thou hast gone up on high" refers to the sacred procession, probably with the Ark of the Covenant, going up Mount

Zion into the Temple, the next lines are of a martial nature. It is not that God has made a captive of captivity, but that he has taken captives (that is, the Israelite armies have), as any modern translation will phrase it. The clauses "and received gifts for men, yea, even for thine enemies" presents an ironic situation. The best translation is that God has received gifts "from men . . . even from thine enemies," as the Prayer Book has it, and as all modern translations read. The reference is to tribute as spoils of war. But the librettist was attracted at this point to the use of the preposition "for" in the King James, and conflated the two texts to arrive at his wording. He wanted to picture the event he is celebrating — the Ascension — as being done on behalf of humanity. The New Revised Standard Version's translation of this vexing verse is:

> You ascended the high mount,
> leading captives in your train
> and receiving gifts from people,
> even from those who rebel against the LORD God's
>     abiding there.

One may compare the Revised English Bible:

> You went up to your dwelling-place on high
> taking captives into captivity;
> everyone brought you tribute;
> no rebel could live in the presence of the LORD God.

One might be driven to the conclusion that the libretto's choice of this passage as a reference to the Ascension of the Messiah might not be as happy as the selection usually is in this work, but there is good precedent, for Ephesians 4:8 also quotes this verse in reference to the Ascension. Here, however, the New Testament text does indeed speak of captivity being made captive, and gifts being given humanity:

> When he ascended on high he made captivity itself a captive,
> and gave gifts to his people.

The New Testament writer (perhaps Paul — the authorship of Ephesians is hotly disputed) is quoting the verse, at least indirectly, from the ancient Greek translation, whose reading is quite different from that of the Hebrew original. The old translators, particularly the King James translators, were apparently influenced in their understanding of the Hebrew Psalm by the New Testament passage, or by the old Greek version, or as is most likely the case, by the Latin Bible intimately familiar to them.

Thus what was originally a liturgical text celebrating the return of God from battle, bringing captives and spoil, and going up to his holy dwelling has become for the New Testament interpreter — and for our oratorio — a reference to Christ's departure from this earth, having accomplished his task of breaking the bonds of those held captive to sin, and bestowing the gift of life. As Psalm 68:20 goes on to say in a passage of clear meaning that well illustrates the continuum between the two readings of verse 18, "Our God is a God of salvation, and to GOD, the Lord, belongs escape from death."

## 37. CHORUS

The Lord gave the word: Great was the company of the preachers. (Psalm 68:11, much modified)

## 38. SOPRANO ARIA

How beautiful are the feet of them that preach the gospel of peace, and bring glad tidings of good things. (Romans 10:15, loosely quoting Isaiah 52:7)

## 39. CHORUS

Their sound is gone out into all lands, and their words

**unto the ends of the world.** *(Romans 10:18b, modified, quoting Psalm 19:4)*

The Book of Acts is the story of the fulfillment of Jesus' Great Commission in Matthew 28:19 to "Go therefore and make disciples of all nations." It is the story of the expansion of what was, with Pentecost and the gift of the Holy Spirit, to become the church, from its primitive beginnings in Jerusalem to the capital city of the Roman Empire. But to convey this part of the story, the oratorio now turns to Psalm 68. Strikingly, however, what the oratorio refers to as "preachers" are in Psalm 68 actually women. In fact, they are not preachers at all, and this word is used in no translation of the Bible, old or modern.

Once again the context is military. God gives the command to battle, and a large number of women bear the glad news of victory. The next line of the psalm is the news they carry: "'The kings of the armies, they flee, they flee!'" (Psalm 68:12). The next verse speaks of the women at home dividing the spoil brought back by Israel's victorious soldiers. Some recent translations obscure the fact that the heralds of the good news are women, but it is clear in the Hebrew. Moreover, it makes perfect cultural sense, for we know that women participated in the victory celebration. After the disaster Pharaoh and his army suffered at the Sea, Moses' sister Miriam sings her song: "Sing to the LORD, for he has triumphed gloriously; horse and rider he has thrown into the sea" (Exodus 15:21). I Samuel 18:6-7 tells how the women of Israel, dancing and playing tambourines, welcomed David back from war, singing, "Saul has killed his thousands, and David his ten thousands."

Several points in Psalm 68 show a relation to the Song of Deborah in Judges 5. Deborah was the woman among the "judges," and chapter 5, an ancient song as difficult in many ways as is Psalm 68, is her song of victory over her enemy Sisera. The song centers on three women: Deborah, Jael (who actually kills Sisera), and Sisera's mother, who worries at her son's failing to return from battle. Her serving maids assure her that the armies are simply dividing the spoil.

Psalm 68, then, appears to be a liturgical piece sung on the occasion of victory, or at a New Year's celebration in the fall, celebrating Israel's prowess in battle. The oratorio, in turn, transforms the celebrations and songs of the dancing girls and women into an army of missionaries, spreading the glad tidings of a victory won by the Messiah over sin and death. This military imagery may seem a strange way to describe the work of missionaries, but it is in line with the thrust of the whole biblical message, the word of the God who wills peace — *shalom* — for his people: "Come, behold the works of the LORD; see what desolations he has brought on the earth. He makes wars cease to the end of the earth; he breaks the bow, and shatters the spear; he burns the shields with fire" (Psalm 46:9).

These early Christian missionaries went out under a divine compulsion, obeying Jesus' Great Commission, and feeling within them what the prophet Jeremiah had felt, "something like a burning fire shut up in my bones" that could not be kept in (Jeremiah 20:9). In his letter to the church at Rome, Paul reflects on the necessity of preachers being sent out to carry the good news, and quotes from Isaiah, "How beautiful are the feet of those who bring good news" (Romans 10:15; Isaiah 52:7).

The Isaiah passage occurs in a context reminiscent of Section 18 in the oratorio, "Rejoice Greatly, O Daughter of Zion," for once again we have a picture of the ruins of Jerusalem hearing the glad news that God is returning to his Holy City, bringing with him the exiled people. "How beautiful upon the mountains are the feet of the messenger who announces peace, who brings good news, who announces salvation, who says to Zion, 'Your God reigns'" (Isaiah 52:7). (In Hebrew, "messenger" is here the masculine singular of the word which occurs in Psalm 68:11 in the feminine plural of Handel's "company of the preachers.") The messenger runs to deliver the news, and the poet concentrates on his swift footfall over the hills, as each pace brings him closer. How welcome his advent! II Samuel 18:24-27 presents a graphic picture of King David anxiously awaiting runners who will bring him news of battle. The image of the messenger's feet must have been familiar in Hebrew poetry. The prophet Nahum uses it: "Look! On the mountains the feet of one who brings good tidings, who proclaims peace!" (Nahum 1:15).

There is also a runner in Psalm 19, a runner who tells of the glory of God. It is the sun, running a joyful course from one end of the heavenly dome that spans the earth to the other (Psalm 19:4-6). The first six verses of this psalm constitute a nature psalm (cf. Psalm 8), in which the created order speaks of God's majesty. Since "the heavens are telling the glory of God" (Psalm 19:1), that divine glory is seen by all the world and all its peoples. It is a revelation that is available to all, bespeaking the wisdom and glory of the Creator. The lights of day and night, the sun, the moon, the stars pour out on humanity cascades of knowledge of God's glory. They speak a language understandable to all. Human beings are provincialized and alienated from one another by their mutually unintelligible languages, but God has not relied solely on the words of mortals to reveal himself. So says Paul: "Ever since the creation of the world his eternal power and divine nature, invisible though they are, have been understood and seen through the things he has made" (Romans 1:20). As the psalmist put it:

> The heavens are telling the glory of God;
>> and the firmament proclaims his handiwork.
> Day to day pours forth speech,
>> and night to night declares knowledge.
> There is no speech, nor are there words;
>> their voice is not heard;
> and yet their voice goes out through all the earth,
>> and their words to the end of the world.
>
> (Psalm 19:1-4a)

The last two lines, as quoted directly from the Book of Common Prayer, are the source for the text of our chorus. In Romans 10:18, as Paul further reflects on the necessity of preaching the gospel, he quotes these two lines of the psalm, making the point that the message of Jesus Christ has been heard all over the world — as Paul knew it, of course — because of the preachers. The good news brought to the nations by the heralds of the King, the Messiah, is read by Paul into the order of creation itself, the saving will of the God who has revealed himself to all in the well-ordered and beneficent sky, in the constancy of the sun which, "like a strong man runs its course with joy" (Psalm 19:5).

~

FROM THE DOMAIN of Heaven, where choirs of angels worship God, the chorus returns us to earth and depicts the host of the Messiah's missionaries, beginning their task of proclaiming to the world the glad tidings that the angels had told the shepherds the night of the Messiah's birth. It is an emboldening chorus. "The Lord gave the word: Great was the company of the preachers."

The soprano's lovely aria is a lyrical meditation on the welcome nature of the message brought by the preachers of the Word. It is the fulfillment of the command given in the first words of the oratorio: "Comfort ye my people." It is the music of peace, the music of comfort, the minister's assurance of pardon.

"Their sound is gone out . . . their sound is gone out . . . their sound is gone out . . . their sound is gone out. . . ." Soprano, alto, tenor, bass: one voice line after another picks up the theme as the chorus sings of the messengers' destination. There is an expansive sweep to the line "and their words unto the ends of the world" that suggests the sun in Psalm 19, running its course with joy from one end of the earth to the other.

## 40. BASS ARIA

**Why do the nations so furiously rage together, and why do the people imagine a vain thing? The kings of the earth rise up, and the rulers take counsel together against the Lord and against his anointed.** *(Psalm 2:1-2, modified)*

## 41. CHORUS

Let us break their bonds asunder, and cast away their yokes from us. *(Psalm 2:3)*

## 42. TENOR RECITATIVE

He that dwelleth in heaven shall laugh them to scorn, the Lord shall have them in derision. *(Psalm 2:4, modified)*

## 43. TENOR ARIA

Thou shalt break them with a rod of iron; thou shalt dash them in pieces like a potter's vessel. *(Psalm 2:9)*

With this sequence we begin our approach to the great Hallelujah chorus, the heavenly enthronement of King Messiah. We will hear him hailed as king over a world that does not acknowledge him as such, as Wonderful Counsellor over a world where the rulers take counsel against him, as Mighty God over a world that holds God in derision, as Everlasting Father of a world that would cast away the easy yoke he lays on it, as Prince of Peace over a world where the nations still furiously rage together. All the angels of God worship him, but this is not the case with his children on earth. The word has gone out into all lands, but it has yet to be heard.

But let us follow this enthronement ceremony from the beginning. The libretto returns us to Psalm 2, one of the ancient enthronement hymns of Israel's kingship, which we have already read in the context of Section 34, "Unto Which of the Angels."

Empire was the order of the day in the ancient world of the Fertile Crescent. Rulers expressed their power by conquering and subjugating other areas. The two great foci of power in that region were Egypt on the western end of the crescent, and the Mesopotamian Valley on the eastern end. Much of ancient Near Eastern history during the Old Testament period consisted of a contest for power between Egypt and whatever power was ascendant in the East — Assyria or Babylonia. The smaller states in between did not stand much of a chance. And that was right where Israel was — caught between two warring giants. Hemmed in by the Mediterranean on the west and the desert to the east, the narrow strip of Israel's territory was traversed by alien armies which often looked on Israel as a prize to be taken, a buffer state to be claimed, while on the march to a larger contest. Slicing across the central highlands of the northern part of the country, from Mt. Carmel on the coast and running southwestward past Mount Megiddo, lay a broad valley, the Valley of Jezreel (Esdraelon in Greek). It was one of few places in the area where opposing armies could meet on level ground, and it was the site of numerous battles. It was there at Megiddo that good King Josiah of Judah died, while trying to block the march of Egyptian armies on their way to meet the Assyrians. So associated was the site with decisive battle that when the apocalyptic writers spoke of a final climactic contest between the forces of good and evil, they conceived of it as taking place at Mount Megiddo — *Har Megiddo* in Hebrew, *Armageddon* in Greek.

Israel and Judah could never hope to hold their own against these stronger states. Only when there was a power vacuum in that theater could they gain strength of their own. Such were the conditions that allowed the rise of David and the "empire" of Solomon. But usually Israel and Judah were in turmoil generated by unrest on the international scene. Often there were political factions at home that advised alliances with one state or the other for protection against what they perceived as a greater danger. Then the prophets would decry the vain attempt to find national salvation from any source other than their God. "Alas for those who go down to Egypt for help and who rely on horses, who trust in chariots because they are many and in horsemen because they are very strong, but do not look to the Holy One of Israel or consult the LORD!" (Isaiah 31:1). "Ephraim [Israel] has become like a dove, silly and without sense; they call upon Egypt, they go to Assyria" (Hosea 7:11). "Oh, rebellious children, says the LORD, who carry out a plan, but not mine; who make an alliance, but against my will, adding sin to sin; who set out to go down to Egypt without asking for my counsel, to take refuge in the protection of Pharaoh, and to seek shelter in the shadow of Egypt" (Isaiah 30:1-2).

Often Israel and Judah preserved their own national life only at the cost of humiliating tribute to a threatening king. Any nation controlling a circle of satellite states could be enriched by such tribute, regularly paid as an indication of submission.

The death of a suzerain king was a signal for revolt. The vassal states saw the opportunity to regain their independence by challenging the power of the new monarch. Each ruler faced the potential task of reconsolidating imperial power in his own name. It was such a rebellion that set in motion the forces leading to the fall of the northern kingdom of Israel. The little nation was under the domination of the Assyrian Empire. When news reached Samaria, the capital city, of the death of Tiglath-Pileser, the Assyrian king, King Hoshea of Israel thought he saw an opportunity. He formally refused tribute to the new monarch, Shalmaneser V, and was quickly attacked. A three-year siege ensued, but in 721 Assyria brought to an end the history of the northern kingdom.

Neither Israel in the north nor Judah in the south was ever a world power. From time to time a respite on the world scene might send a Judean king on a modest adventure, capturing a town or so in the region, but no mighty monarch ever trembled in fear at the prospect of a threat from the House of David in Jerusalem.

Why then does Psalm 2 read as it does? It is clearly an enthronement psalm, to be sung at the installation of a new Judean king, or perhaps, as some scholars suggest, at an annual ritual reenthronment at a New Year's festival in the fall, celebrating as well the ritual enthronement of God in the Temple, as we considered in Section 33, "Lift Up Your Heads."

As the psalm begins, we are asked to contemplate a situation in which the world's rulers are plotting to overcome the sway of the King of Judah: "Why do the nations conspire, and the peoples plot in vain?" (v. 1). Of course their plots are futile, for they are actually plotting against the God of Judah. To conspire against God's anointed king is to conspire against God. But look at the senseless scene: "The kings of the earth set themselves, and the rulers take counsel together against the LORD and his anointed, saying, 'Let us burst their bonds asunder, and cast their cords from us'" (vv. 2-3). Ah, they see their chance. A new king comes to the throne in Jerusalem, and the subject peoples plot together to overthrow his rule.

The scene now shifts to heaven. The Lord, high above the absurd, useless conniving of these earthly rulers, can only be amused: "He who sits in the heavens laughs; the LORD has them in derision" (v. 4). But he will put an end to their plots. "Then he will speak to them in his wrath, and terrify them in his fury, saying, 'I have set my king on Zion, my holy hill'" (vv. 5-6). God will be faithful to his covenant with David.

God speaks now to the king. "You are my son; today I have begotten you. Ask of me, and I will make the nations your heritage, and the ends of the earth your possession. You shall break them with a rod of iron, and dash them in pieces like a potter's vessel" (vv. 7-9). The reference to iron is particularly potent; the Iron Age may have begun in Israel only shortly before the time of David. The imagery of broken pottery is common in the Bible.

So God offers his Anointed One mastery of all lands, of the ends of the world. It is possible that the themes used in this enthronement liturgy were standard in the ancient Near East and that the poet is drawing on a foreign model. But this hardly explains the fact that there is no point in the history of Israel or Judah when such statements would have been literally appropriate, when subjugated kings were waiting for a chance to rebel against an overlord in Zion. Is this a religious expression of mere wishful thinking?

Probably not. The Israelites were aware of their situation. They knew the precariousness of any independence they enjoyed, and they knew their weakness compared with real imperial might. But their God, they believed, was ultimately in control of historical forces. This is the God who uses governments for his own purposes, who says through the prophet Isaiah, "Ah, Assyria, the rod of my anger — the club in their hands is my fury'" (Isaiah 10:5). This is the God who, Amos says, guides the destiny of all nations, not just that of Israel: "Did I not bring Israel up from the land of Egypt, and the Philistines from Caphtor and the Arameans from Kir?" (Amos 9:7). And this is the God who has installed his Anointed King on Zion.

It is only faith that could see the God of little Israel, little Judah, as active in the swirling currents of history. One whose attention is focused only on the immediate political sequence of cause and effect would see no such evidence. To such a person the claims of the King of Judah in Psalm 2 render him a silly pretender. But the person who saw divine purpose in the counsels and actions of human agencies would perceive a divine destiny in the Davidic kingship, in the office of the Anointed One who has not only been raised by God to the kingship, but who has submitted himself to that God, and subjected himself to God's purposes. The acclamation of the King in such grandiose phrases as found in this psalm represent nothing less than an expression of communal faith, of confidence and hope that something grander is here being proclaimed than the immediate influence of Jerusalem's royal court. The royal is taking on an eschatological cast; it is directing itself away from the present, or out of the present into the future. Their God has entered into covenant with his people and he is loyal to his word. He will maintain his covenant with David. So fierce was this faith that even after the complete collapse of the kingdom, it survived in the form of the hope that God would yet send an anointed one, a Messiah, to restore the kingdom and reassume the throne of David. The book of Daniel, which probably dates from the second century B.C., expresses it:

> The kingship and dominion
>> and the greatness of the kingdoms under the whole heaven
>> shall be given to the people of the holy ones of the Most High;
> their kingdom shall be an everlasting kingdom,
>> and all dominions shall serve and obey them.
>
> (Daniel 7:27)

By the time, long after the exile, that the praises of Israel were collected and organized into the Book of Psalms which we now know, these royal psalms could have had no meaning for the compilers other than the messianic.

And so in the oratorio *Messiah,* Christian voices from a world in which the word has gone forth but not been received sing the words of eschatological hope latent in the ancient psalm. Messiah has come, but his earthly sway is no more evident than the imperial power of the King of Judah. Faith is here being expressed that this one who submitted himself to God's saving purposes, even to death on a cross, is the ruler of all humanity. Peter and John remembered these words from Psalm 2 in reflecting on the fate of the earthly Jesus at the hands of Herod and Pilate (Acts 4:25-26). It had all worked in God's plan for the emboldening of the preachers. They spoke these words in prayer, and "when they had prayed, the place in which they gathered together was shaken; and they were all filled with the Holy Spirit and spoke the word of God with boldness" (Acts 4:31).

~

A FURIOUS, frenetic accompaniment underlies the bass aria "Why Do the Nations?" but the vocal line strides across it with confident authority. The proclamation towers over the ceaseless frenzy of the background like an invincible walled city against a milling army of would-be attackers.

The chorus speaks for the rebels, expressing their futile dream in long, graceful runs on the word "away," thinking they can rid themselves of the claims of God and his Messiah.

In contrast to the extended chorus of rebellious kings, the tenor's brief recitative simply tells of God's lofty derision toward their efforts.

The tenor's aria then turns to God's wrath, angry words to an angry accompaniment reducing whole kingdoms to fields of broken crockery.

And so we are ready, looking across the present into the future, to sing the Messiah's enthronement song in "the assurance of things hoped for, the conviction of things not seen" (Hebrew 11:1). God's rule is established, and we are ready for the great chorus.

## 44. CHORUS

**Hallelujah, for the Lord God Omnipotent reigneth, Hallelujah!** *(Revelation 19:6b, modified)*

**The Kingdom of this world is become the Kingdom of our Lord, and of his Christ, and he shall reign for ever and ever, Hallelujah!** *(Revelation 11:15b)*

**King of Kings, and Lord of Lords, and he shall reign for ever and ever, Hallelujah!** *(Revelation 19:16b, modified)*

Christians, by A.D. 95 or so, were somewhat in the position of ancient Judah in the political context of the Fertile Crescent. They held on to a minority faith in the face of horrendous external stress, sensitive to the precarious nature of their existence as a movement, even at times of their own personal survival. But their situation was even more attenuated than that of a single small state. For this was no little kingdom of Christians huddling together for mutual support in an obscure geographical corner. These were people spread over the Roman world. They were Judeans, and Syrians, and Egyptians; Gauls, Illyrians, Cretans; people from Malta and Iberia and Galatia, Africa and Asia. They were tiny minorities everywhere, trying to live lives of submission to a heavenly king in the midst of the surrounding pagan cultures. The threat of apostasy, of assimilation, of the gradual dissolution of their faith was always real.

The world had always been an alien environment for the young Christian movement, but by the nineties it had turned hostile. There was something annoying about their worship of only one God. There was something disloyal, unpatriotic about their consequent refusal to worship the genius of the Emperor. To most peoples of the Empire this was little more than a gesture, like saluting the flag or saying the Pledge of Allegiance, but Christians took it more literally and seriously. The state became alarmed about the spread of the faith among so many peoples and nationalities. There was an organization growing among these Christians, a *church,* and it knew no provincial boundaries. Like the Empire itself, it thought of itself as worldwide in scope. It was the only organization that in this way resembled the Roman state, and it thereby constituted a potential threat to established authority.

There had been persecutions. Most of these had been local affairs, but some of them were truly vicious. To a hapless Christian believer, wishing to give witness to his or her faith, the force of the Roman Empire coming down must have seemed like a world caving in. Many did elect to give their witness to the point of suffering death; we know these witnesses by the Greek word for a witness: martyrs.

The presumption of a small Near Eastern state installing a new king that they hailed as powerful over all other kings was of a different order from isolated communities of Christian witnesses suffering impending death and annihilation. But the martyrs, and those who knew they might be called on to face martyrdom, were stalwart in their conviction that, Rome notwithstanding, God ruled.

Visionary authors among their number turned to the Jewish genre of apocalyptic to express their faith. They came to see the climax of personal and community reckoning as a presaging of a climactic struggle between good and evil, between God and Satan, in which God and his Anointed — the Messiah — would emerge victorious. In the vivid images of traditional apocalyptic one such writer — we know him as John — painted this faith in the book of Revelation. Evil has gone as far as it can go. The Roman Empire is the dominion of Satan, and God must soon challenge its haughty arrogance. The worlds of space and time dissolve in the visions described. Cataclysms are conjured up that can be expressed only in such earthly images as hail and fire and blood and vicious fantastic creatures. Such, indeed, must be the wrath of God on a sinfully defiant world, the logical extension of what the prophets as far back as Amos had been calling the Day of the Lord.

In the midst of this shaking of the heavens and the earth, the sea and the dry land, an angel blows a trumpet, and voices are heard, loud voices from Heaven, proclaiming the accession of the King from the line of David: "The kingdom of this world has become the kingdom of our Lord and of his Messiah, and he will reign forever and ever" (Revelation 11:15). There is a vision of the fall of Rome, pictured as the ancient and fallen city of Babylon, and there are more voices, the sound of which reverberate like thunder, like the sound of waterfalls: "Hallelujah! For the Lord our God the Almighty reigns" (Revelation 19:6). Now heaven opens, and the Messiah himself, the Word of God, comes forth on a white charger, to fulfill the messianic role of defeating the enemies of God's people, "to strike down the nations, and . . . rule them with a rod of iron" (Revelation 19:15). Inscribed on Messiah's robe and thigh is the device: "King of Kings and Lord of Lords" (Revelation 19:16). Following the victory, Satan is vanquished, a new heaven and earth appear, and the saints of God begin their eternal life with God.

In words such as these, early Christians losing their footing in the world found the stability of hope, the assurance that though they had refused to worship the beast of Rome and well might die as a consequence, they were on the victorious side. God would yet show himself faithful to his faithful people by fidelity to his covenant with David: the Messiah will reign in a kingdom where all other allegiances melt away.

Rome did not fall. Not anytime soon. And evil had not reached a climax. The horrors of the twentieth century surpass anything experienced or conceived of in the nightmares of the first. But when we read in Revelation of the four horsemen and the seven trumpets and the seven bowls and the wars and epidemics and famines of the end time, we are blind not to see ourselves in its pages. The author was not predicting events of the twentieth century. He was writing of things ultimate. He saw them impinging on his own time and we may see them impinging on ours. These are images to warn and to give comfort to every age, for each generation is always living its own end time. Here is poetic imagery of a high order put to the service of the church in every age of witnessing to the reality and deadly seriousness of sin and evil, and to the reality and inevitability of God's victory over it all.

Comment on the music of the chorus would be superfluous. It is easily accessible and can be appreciated by all with an appropriate sense of wonder.

But the grand force of the chorus is lost by the unfortunate custom of performing a so-called "Christmas section" of the oratorio (Part I) and concluding with Hallelujah. Here the chorus makes no sense at all. Handel's librettist produced a magnificent structure of words, with everything in the right place. Handel himself was an experienced composer of opera and had a genuine sense of the dramatic. In conceiving of the great chorus as Messiah's enthronement on high after his victory over death, both men knew what they were doing.

# PART III

## 45. Soprano Aria

I know that my Redeemer liveth, and that he shall stand at the latter day upon the earth. And though worms destroy this body, yet in my flesh shall I see God. *(Job 19:25-26, modified)*

For now is Christ risen from the dead, the first fruits of them that sleep. *(I Corinthians 15:20, modified)*

## 46. Chorus

Since by man came death, by man came also the resurrection of the dead. For as in Adam all die, even so in Christ shall all be made alive. *(I Corinthians 15:21-22)*

Ancient Israel had an extensive body of law, but it had no police force. Yet without enforcement, law is meaningless. The king could see that acts against the state were punished, but crimes against persons were left to the vengeance of the offended family or clan. It fell to a person's next-of-kin to serve as an avenger on behalf of an injured relative. For the time being, let us call this person the *goel;* that is the Hebrew term.

The law provided that for cases of manslaughter, accidental killings, certain cities of refuge should be provided. The guilty party could flee there for sanctuary until such time as formal proceedings could be initiated: "The cities shall be for you a refuge from the *goel,* so that the slayer may not die until there is a trial before the congregation" (Numbers 35:12).

The history of the northern kingdom of Israel is one of bloody *coups d'etat.* We are told of one involving Zimri, who murders King Elah and installs himself as king. He then killed off all of Elah's kindred: "he did not leave him a single male of his *goels* or his friends" (I Kings 16:11). There was no one left to avenge the murder.

If a man died childless, it was the obligation of his *goel* to marry the widow. Ruth, the young Moabite widow, attempts to seduce Boaz in the belief that he is her *goel* (Ruth 3:7-9). But she is mistaken. Boaz explains, "It is true that I am a *goel*, [but] there is another *goel* more closely related than I. . . . In the morning, if he will act as *goel* for you, good. . . . If he is not willing . . . I will act as *goel* for you" (Ruth 3:12-13). The man who is nearest of kin waives his rights, and Boaz marries Ruth. They have a son, who would be David's grandfather. This marriage custom is also reflected in the strange account of Tamar's seduction of her father-in-law Judah in Genesis 38, as well as in the question the Sadducees put to Jesus in Mark 12:18-27.

The book of Job, the literary Everest of the Bible, is the story of an innocent sufferer. Job is a righteous man who has lost all his wealth and all his children and has been personally afflicted with a painful, loathsome disease. Three friends appear, and counsel him that he is suffering as punishment for sin. The reader knows that this is not true, and so does Job. He protests his innocence. As his conversation with the three men goes on, Job's words grow shriller and closer to blasphemy, as he accuses God of injustice. At one point he describes his desolation:

> "He has put my family far from me, and my acquaintances are wholly estranged from me. My relatives and my close friends have failed me. . . . I am loathsome to my own family. . . . All my intimate friends abhor me, and those whom I loved have turned against me. . . . Have pity on me, have pity on me, O you my friends, for the hand of God has touched me. . . . O that my words were written down! O that they were inscribed in a book! . . . For I know that my *goel* lives . . ." (Job 19:13-25).

He knows that somewhere there is someone to serve as his avenger, as his vindicator. While it is possible to read this in such a way that Job is referring to a human figure, the *goel* the poet has in mind is surely God.

Israelite thought did not conceive of God as a philosophical abstraction. Theirs was a personal God, who interacted with human beings. Any human language is inadequate to describe God, but the biblical writers chose the inadequacies of human analogies rather than the inadequacies of depersonalized abstraction, even if this meant speaking of God as a male. God is a warrior; he is a father; he is a king; he is a *goel* — next-of-kin who vindicates his people. This picture is found in the Psalms: "Let the words of my mouth and the meditation of my heart be acceptable to you, O LORD, my rock and my *goel* — my redeemer" (Psalm 19:14). God as the Redeemer, the *goel,* of his people is particularly associated with the exilic Isaiah: "Our Redeemer — the LORD of hosts is his name — is the Holy One of Israel" (Isaiah 47:4). The word *goel* is applied to God fourteen times in Isaiah 40–66, once in Jeremiah, twice in the Psalms, perhaps once in Proverbs, and here at Job 19:25. The word "Redeemer" is not found in the New Testament, although salvation is described as redemption several times.

Job 19:25-26 forms part of the text for the soprano aria. The first line, "I know that my Redeemer lives," is the only simple part of these two verses. The Hebrew text is here in a bad state of disrepair, and it is very difficult indeed to extract sense from it. There are probably no two verses in all the Bible where the various translations go in such disparate directions as here. A measure of the difficulty can be seen by looking at the italicized words in the King James text. Italic type in the King James Version is a device used by the translators to alert the reader to the fact that these words are not in the original text of the Bible; the translators have inserted them to make sense. Ordinarily this is a routine business of inserting articles and conjunctions, but look at the words in our passage which have been inserted, which do not occur in the Hebrew text at all: "For I know *that* my redeemer liveth, and *that* he shall stand at the latter *day* upon the earth: And *though* after my skin *worms* destroy this *body,* yet in my flesh shall I see God." There is nothing in the text about a day, about worms, or even about a body. And there are several other problems, such as that the word "earth" really means "dust," and that "in my flesh" can be translated "without my flesh."

These verses have been referred to earlier in the context of speaking of the Hebrew concept of life after death. It is conceivable that the poet of Job is speaking of Job's being vindicated after his death, but it may not be likely, since the concept is nowhere else referred to in the book, and since the original intent of these two verses appears to be hopelessly obscure.

The context in the book of Job is one thing, but the context in Handel's *Messiah* is quite another. Here the scene has shifted from the heavenly enthronement of Part II to the earthly scene. The believer confesses faith that she has a redeemer, a vindicator to plead her cause, who will eventually appear on earth (a reference to the Second Coming of Christ). Even though her earthly remains are thoroughly decomposed, at that time she will be resurrected, in the body, to see God.

Resurrected — as was Christ. The remainder of the aria derives from I Corinthians 15, the passage where Paul gives his most thorough discussion of the idea of resurrection. Indeed, it is our earliest such witness to the Resurrection, since Paul is the earliest of all the New Testament writers. The church at Corinth, a bustling seaport city in Greece, had been founded by Paul, but the congregation came to be rent by controversy, disputes over matters moral and theological. First Corinthians (which was not in fact Paul's first letter to them; that letter has been lost — see I Corinthians 5:9) was written at least partially in response to a communication to Paul from the church, asking about certain matters.

One of the problems in Corinth had to do with the question of the resurrection of the dead. We do not know the precise nature of the problems there, but in some manner some in the congregation did not feel that a resurrected life awaited all believers. The fifteenth chapter addresses this. Paul gives an account of appearances made by the risen Christ himself, insisting that Christ *has* been raised from the dead, but Christ, in his resurrection, was "the first fruits of those who have died," "fallen asleep." The term "first fruits" is a technical term from the Jewish sacrificial system. The first produce of the fields and orchards were to be dedicated to God; this offering insured the blessing of God on the rest of the crops (Proverbs 3:9-10). The firstborn male child in a family was also to be dedicated to God, but redeemed, bought back

(Exodus 13:12-16). This ritual recalled that the firstborn of the Hebrews were saved on the night when the plague of death struck the firstborn of Egypt. Israel itself is thought of as special to the Lord, and is described as the firstborn: "Israel was holy to the LORD, the first fruits of his harvest" (Jeremiah 2:3). So also was the king of the House of David described. In one of the royal psalms God says of the king, "I will make him the firstborn, the highest of the kings of earth. Forever I will keep my steadfast love for him, and my covenant with him will stand firm" (Psalm 89:27-28).

In this imagery, then, the resurrection of Christ is the first fruits, the guarantee of the harvest to come, of the resurrection of all who believe.

"For since death came through a human being, the resurrection of the dead has also come through a human being" (I Corinthians 15:21). Paul refers here to Adam and to Christ. Paul assumes the rabbinic doctrine that all humanity was involved in Adam's sin and punishment, his willful disobedience of God and consignment to mortality. But, he reasons, in the same way deliverance from death has come about by the involvement of Christ in all humanity. Insofar as we share human nature with Adam, we die. But insofar as we accept the claims of Christ, we shall be made alive. The argument is a logical extension of Paul's image of the church as the Body of Christ. All those who are in Christ are members of his body. As such we share in both his death and resurrection, as is pictured in baptism:

We have been buried with him by baptism into death, so that, just as Christ was raised from the dead by the glory of the Father, so we too might walk in newness of life. For if we have been united with him in a death like his, we will certainly be united with him in a resurrection like his. (Romans 6:4-5)

~

THE SHIFT in key from the D of the Hallelujah Chorus to the E of the soprano aria is striking. A higher level of human existence has been reached with the resurrection of Christ. The music flows with soft, gentle strength. The conquest is won; the conflict is in the past. Safe, all danger in the past, the soprano now serenely proclaims the resurrection of the body.

The chorus makes the application to all humanity, at first whispering gravely the primordial sentence of death, brought on by humankind, then joyously exploding into an *allegro* of resurrected life.

## 47. BASS RECITATIVE

Behold, I tell you a mystery; we shall not all sleep, but we shall all be chang'd, in a moment, in the twinkling of an eye, at the last trumpet. (*I Corinthians 15:51-52, modified*)

## 48. BASS ARIA

The trumpet shall sound, and the dead shall be rais'd incorruptible, and we shall be chang'd. For this corruptible must put on incorruption, and this mortal must put on immortality. (*I Corinthians 15:52-53*)

## 49. ALTO RECITATIVE

Then shall be brought to pass the saying that is written, Death is swallow'd up in victory. (*I Corinthians 15:54b*)

## 50. ALTO AND TENOR DUET

O death, where is thy sting? O grave, where is thy victory? The sting of death is sin, and the strength of sin is the law. (*I Corinthians 15:55-56*)

## 51. Chorus

**But thanks be to God, who giveth us the victory through our Lord Jesus Christ.** *(I Corinthians 15:57)*

*"Marana tha!"* "Our Lord, come!" The words are Aramaic, the language of New Testament Palestine, but Paul quotes them in a book written in Greek (I Corinthians 16:22). This is surely one of the most ancient prayers of the Christian church, going back to the time when the faith was composed mainly of Christian Jews living in Palestine. But Paul quotes it to his Gentile audience; it must have been perceived as important. The book of Revelation closes with a form of it: "Come, Lord Jesus!" (Revelation 22:20).

The belief that Christ will come again, this next time in decisive judgment, has always been a feature of Christian doctrine. At some times and among some groups the expectation has been more vivid than at other times and among other groups. For those Protestants who are much concerned with signs of an impending end, the Second Coming plays a large part in study and preaching. But even in other Christian circles the doctrine of the Second Coming is confessed every Sunday in the Apostles' Creed: "seated at the right hand of the Father Almighty from whence he shall return to judge the living and the dead," or in the Nicene Creed: "He shall come again in glory to judge the living and the dead."

The roots of the idea are in Jewish apocalyptic writings which speak occasionally of a Son of Man who appears out of the sea or out of the clouds to act as God's agent in judgment at the end time. Whatever Jesus may have meant in referring to himself as the Son of Man — the question is fiercely debated among scholars — the fact remains that the gospels contain a number of sayings in which the Son of Man as an apocalyptic figure of judgment is mentioned; all of these are in the words of Jesus. "Those who are ashamed of me and of my words in this adulterous and sinful generation, of them the Son of Man will also be ashamed when he comes in the glory of his Father with the holy angels" (Mark 8:38). In Mark 13, the "Little Apocalypse,"

"The sun will be darkened, and the moon will not give its light, and the stars will be falling from heaven, and the powers in the heavens will be shaken. Then they will see 'the Son of Man coming in clouds' with great power and glory. Then he will send out the angels, and gather his elect from the four winds, from the ends of the earth to the ends of heaven." (Mark 13:24-27)

At the only point in the gospel story where Jesus specifically and clearly admits to being the Messiah, he quickly deflects the discussion to the Son of Man: "Again the high priest asked him, 'Are you the Messiah, the Son of the Blessed One?' Jesus said, 'I am, and you will see the Son of Man seated at the right hand of the Power, and coming with the clouds of heaven'" (Mark 14:61-62).

What the historical Jesus meant when speaking of the Son of Man is an interesting and vexing question, but there is no doubt whatever what the scriptural writers mean by it and what the primitive Christian church understood by the title. Jesus was the Christ — the Messiah — and they interpreted him in the light of the guidance of the ancient prophecies and psalms dealing with the kingship and the covenant with David. These Scriptures, they said, interpret Jesus. Jesus is the Suffering Servant. The passages in Isaiah that speak of the servant of the Lord who innocently suffers on behalf of others interpret for us who Jesus is. And Jesus is the Son of Man — after all, he used the term himself — and the traditions, even though not in the Hebrew Scriptures, that speak of the Son of Man's coming at the end of time to judge the world also interpret who Jesus is. Any of these lines of thought, these religious motifs, can be studies in their Jewish context alone, where they never merge. But in Christian faith they did merge. They converged on Jesus, who was then seen and confessed by Christians as the fulfillment of all these lines of expectation.

Given the fact that Jesus, in his earthly life, did not fulfill the expectations regarding the Messiah, and given the fact that the remembered words of Jesus himself spoke of his return as Son of Man, it was natural and inevitable that the belief in the Second Coming should develop. "And just as it is appointed for mortals to die once, and after that the judgment, so Christ, having been offered once to bear the sins of many, will appear a second time, not to deal with sin, but to save those who are eagerly waiting for him" (Hebrews 9:27-28). "What sort of persons ought you to be in leading lives of holiness and godliness, waiting for and hastening the coming of the day of God, because of which the heavens will be set ablaze and be dissolved, and the elements will melt with fire?" (II Peter 3:11-12).

This idea of the Lord's return to earth was joined with the belief in the resurrection of the dead. Paul had written earlier, in what is probably his earliest surviving letter:

> We who are alive, who are left until the coming of the Lord, will by no means precede those who have died. For the Lord himself, with a cry of command, with the archangel's call and with the sound of God's trumpet, will descend from heaven, and the dead in Christ shall rise first. Then we who are alive, who are left, will be caught up in the clouds together with them to meet the Lord in the air. . . . (I Thessalonians 4:15-17)

This was such a vivid expectation that many of the first Christian generation thought they would be the last generation. Paul seemed to share this thought. In the text of the bass recitative, which begins a sequence based on I Corinthians 15, he says, "Listen, I will tell you a mystery! We shall not all die, but we will all be changed, in a moment, in the twinkling of an eye, at the last trumpet" (I Corinthians 15:51-52). At this last trumpet blast — which does not mean the last in a series, but a trumpet that marks the end, finality — the living will be transformed as will the dead in Christ, and it sounds as if Paul expects to be among the transformed living at the time. They could recall a saying of Jesus: "There are some standing here who will not taste death before they see the Son of Man coming in his kingdom" (Matthew 16:28).

Here and there in the New Testament are passages such as these that describe in pictorial images the final moment, but there is not a great consistency among them. Those who attempt to distill from these passages a narrative of future events are predestined to differences of opinion because of the nature of the sources. When biblical writers borrowed from the resources of apocalyptic to talk to human and earthly finality, they were using language with which they were at home. They did not employ the vocabulary of philosophy with its abstractions, nor did they use the literal, precise canons of modern journalism and historiography. They used the vibrant colors and amplified sounds of enhanced narrative to infuse their picture of the end time with a sense of urgency. Their goal was a riveting effect on the imagination, and consistency was not one of the canons adopted toward that goal.

A built-in problem of Christian evangelism is the maintaining of a sense of urgency in the face of ultimate matters after two millennia of existence in a world in which the Kingdom of God has yet to come with power. The tension is seen in the sayings of Jesus dealing with the Kingdom; sometimes he speaks of it as if it is yet to come, sometimes as if it were present. He thinks of it as future, but so close, so impending, that the only human option is "Repent, for the kingdom of heaven has come near" (Matthew 3:2). Christian preaching has for centuries been charged with that tension between the already here and the not yet come. Every generation is its own last generation, facing its own call to repentance in face of its own impending end, its own threat of judgment, its own coming of the Kingdom.

Some Christians see the Second Coming of Christ as a literal event, to happen at some specific moment in the future. Other Christians see the Second Coming as a metaphor, a symbolic statement of the pervasive force of the constant inbreaking of God's Kingdom into history, working toward the betterment of the social structures of this world. However the poetic images be interpreted, the irreducible minimum of the doctrine of the Second Coming is that just as the beginning of this world, of this history, and of our lives was in the hands of God, so too is the end of this world, of this history, and of our lives. It imbues the living of our lives and the conduct of our history with a seriousness that can come from no other ground than the faith that decisions made here are of eternal import.

The bass aria, "The Trumpet Shall Sound," from I Corinthians 15:52-53, goes on to express the idea of entrance into everlasting life as a change of nature, for the living as well as the dead. The great creeds of the church have always expressed this hope in terms of "the resurrection of the body" rather than "the immortality of the soul." These are different concepts, although not altogether mutually exclusive.

The immortality of the soul can be understood — and was understood by some lines of ancient thought — to mean that the soul, as distinct from the body, is by its very nature immortal. Its immortality is a physical property, but the return of the soul to its origin in divinity does not necessarily imply the survival of individual consciousness after death. As the stuff of the body becomes one with the earth, the lighter stuff of the soul simply becomes one with God.

Resurrection of the body affirms the survival of the person's own self, and attributes this survival to God's miraculous intervention rather than to the operation of natural law.

It is true that the literature and vocabulary of the Old Testament do not make the same sharp distinction between body and soul that some Greek thought does, but it is not true to say that the Israelites could not and did not conceive of individual existence apart from the body. Everyone knew that dead bodies decayed and returned to earth, but still people could speak of existence, however shadowy, in a land of the dead, Sheol. Between the testaments, when Jewish and Greek thought came into closer contact, some Jews found the idea of the soul useful in formulating their developing beliefs about the nature of the afterlife. Yet Jews could not compromise the sovereignty of God the Creator; this was affirmed by insisting on the transition from this life to the next as resurrection, or as Paul puts it in our text here, change. We need not try to deny our mortality — death is no illusion — but immortality awaits us in "the sure and certain hope of the Resurrection."

To some ancients, as well as to some moderns, the resurrection of the body may have seemed a crass, ignoble, less than spiritual notion. But it is the way in which biblical faith insists on immortality as the transformed continuance of personhood, not as mystical dissolution into some divine vastness, or as reincarntion at a later time into different selves.

And so the alto begins her recitative, "Then the saying that is written will be fulfilled: 'Death has been swallowed up in victory'" (I Corinthians 15:54).

Paul's quotation is from Isaiah 25, from a context that is worth examining. It occurs in the so-called Little Apocalypse of Isaiah 24–25. Chapter 24 ends with a picture of God's enthronement on Zion: "Then the moon will be abashed, and the sun ashamed; for the LORD of hosts will reign on Mount Zion and in Jerusalem . . ." (Isaiah 24:23). On Mount Zion God will prepare a banquet for all nations — a theme common enough in apocalyptic literature. Here is a picturing of the prophetic vision come true, that the peoples of the world will come to the Lord, symbolized by their pilgrimage to Zion. God's gift of life is pictured in the image of goodliness: "How precious is your steadfast love, O God! All people may take refuge in the shadow of your wings. They feast on the abundance of your house, and you give them drink from the river of your delights. For with you is the fountain of life . . ." (Psalm 36:7-9). Jesus refers to a great messianic banquet: "Many will come from east and west and will eat with Abraham and Isaac and Jacob in the kingdom of heaven . . ." (Matthew 8:11). In Revelation it becomes the marriage supper of the Lamb (Revelation 19:9). It is this which the Lord's Supper anticipates: "I will never again drink of this fruit of the vine until that day when I drink it new with you in my Father's kingdom" (Matthew 26:24).

Here is how our Isaiah passage pictures the bounty:

"On this mountain the LORD of hosts will make for all peoples
    a feast of rich food, a feast of well-aged wines
of rich food filled with marrow,
    of well-aged wines strained clear.
And he will destroy on this mountain
    the shroud that is cast over all peoples,
    the sheet that is spread over all nations;

138

he will swallow up death forever.
Then the Lord GOD will wipe away the tears
from all faces. . . ."

(Isaiah 25:6-8)

The shroud over the peoples is death. When it is pulled from their faces, their tears will be wiped away. Revelation also carries through with this theme: "He will wipe away every tear from their eyes. Death will be no more" (Revelation 21:4). God will swallow up death forever, just as it is the grave that usually swallows up its victims. A psalmist gives thanks for God's rescuing him from enemies who "would have swallowed us up alive" (Psalm 124:3). Proverbs pictures the wicked waiting in ambush for the righteous, murmuring to each other, "Come with us, let us lie in wait for blood . . . like Sheol let us swallow them alive, and whole, like those who go down to the Pit" (Proverbs 1:11-12). Isaiah described the punishment to come on his people, "Therefore, Sheol has enlarged its appetite and opened its mouth beyond measure" (Isaiah 5:14).

But in our passage it is Sheol itself, Death, that is swallowed up. "Forever," says Isaiah; "in victory," writes Paul. The discrepancy here goes back to the ancient versions. The ancient Greek translation of the Old Testament which we have referred to a number of times was not the only one made. There were a few minor ones as well, and one of those here reads "He will drown death in victory." Paul evidently knew the Isaiah passage in a form that read "victory," and it is that form which it serves his purposes to quote.

Communion with God is possible; eternal life is attainable. Not through anything we humans have done, but because of what God has done. It is not that an angry God has been appeased and mollified. It is rather that God himself has vanquished the minions of death. It is a victory that has been won, but won for us by another. Herein is the "sure and certain hope of the Resurrection unto eternal life."

The duet for alto and tenor constitutes a taunt song over the destruction of death. We continue with the passage from I Corinthians 15 with the questions, "Where, O death, is your victory? Where,

139

O death, is your sting?" The textual history of this verse in the manuscript tradition is quite complicated, and there is no need to enter it here except simply to say that this is the explanation for the variations one will find between Handel's text and the various translations of I Corinthians 15:55.

More interesting are the differences between Paul's wording and that of the eighth-century prophet Hosea, whom he is loosely quoting. In the context of Hosea, a wrathful God is determined to punish his sinful people. God asks two rhetorical questions:

Shall I ransom them from the power of Sheol?
Shall I redeem them from Death?

(Hosea 13:14)

The obvious answer is "No, I shall not!" So he calls for death like a hunter whistling for his dogs:

O Death, where are your plagues?
O Sheol, where is your destruction?

Bring them on, God says. "Compassion is hid from my eyes" (Hosea 13:14).

Paul's word "victory" is surely chosen by him instead of "plagues" to tie in the thought with the passage from Isaiah he has just quoted. His mention of "sting" is the reading of the ancient Greek translation. The word used there has a broad reference; and translation is forced to be unfortunately specific. The word may refer to a cattle-driver's prod, or to an instrument of torture, or to the sting of a creature like a scorpion. Death is no longer our driver, our tormentor; it has been defanged and rendered harmless.

Paul's use of the passage is remarkable. Violently wrenched from its context, he makes the prophet's words say the precise opposite of what Hosea intended. A summons from death to come do its worst has become a triumphal taunt over death's defeat. The difference is that in Paul's context an altogether different signal, a different summons has been heard. The last trumpet has sounded and the dead have been raised. The trumpet that calls forth the dead and summons the living is the trumpet announcing Messiah's ultimate victory.

The sentence "The sting of death is sin, and the power of sin is the law" (I Corinthians 15:56) seems to fit so poorly into Paul's context that some scholars have assumed it to be a later insertion into the text from another hand. Probably not. More likely, Paul, who customarily thinks faster than he writes, has just had this thought, which he wants to be sure to get in. It is quite typical of his thinking. Speaking of scorpions and cobras, he reasons, the sting of death I have just mentioned is sin, and its power is in the Law. The background to this is in Romans 7:7-25, where Paul argues that although the Law — the Law of Moses — is holy and just, it is the Law that makes us aware of the true nature of sin. But Law does not give us the ability to resist sin. Consequently we must live under its just condemnation. It sets up a wrenching conflict: One wants to do right, but cannot.

> So I find it to be a law that when I want to do what is good, evil lies close at hand. For I delight in the law of God in my inmost self, but I see in my members another law at war with the law of my mind, making me captive to the law of sin that dwells in my members. Wretched man that I am! Who will rescue me from this body of death? Thanks be to God through Jesus Christ our Lord! (Romans 7:21-25)

Here in the passage sung in the duet, Paul's thought is drawn to the Law, the Torah he loves as a Jew but the demands of which he finds himself as a sinner unable to keep. But he then bursts out into thanksgiving, just as in the Romans passage, to the grace of God in Christ who frees him from the dilemma. His thanksgiving is the text for the chorus: "But thanks be to God, who gives us the victory through our Lord Jesus Christ" (I Corinthians 15:57). Victory over sin and death itself through Jesus Christ. Paul uses the word "victory" only three times in all his letters; all three occurrences are in this one passage.

THE BASS RECITATIVE that begins this sequence opens on the same interval, the same word "Behold," that began the alto's announcement of the mystery of the Virgin Birth in Part I. He whispers in our ear until he tells us that we shall be changed. Then the sudden leap from low A to high B with only two quick sixteenth notes in between on F# grabs us by the arm and forces us to see the transformation, the change. It will happen at that last trumpet.

Now we do hear the trumpet sound, in an instrumental solo rare in this work. It is the sound of the trumpet in the *Tuba Mirum* triplet of the *Dies Irae* sequence in the traditional Requiem mass: "The trumpet spreads its awesome sound through the regions of the dead, calling everyone before the throne." And then the bass begins to sing out the words summoning the dead to life.

## 52. SOPRANO ARIA

**If God be for us, who can be against us? Who shall lay anything to the charge of God's elect? It is God that justifieth, who is he that condemneth? It is Christ that died, yea rather, that is risen again, who is at the right hand of God, who maketh intercession for us.** *(Romans 8:31b, 33-34)*

Victory? What victory? We hear the pounding hoofbeats of the ghastly steeds of the four horsemen, our ears ring with the sound of the seven trumpets, we are inundated by the contents of the seven bowls emptied on earth. We need not even look to global problems like wars, epidemics, and famine. Closer to home we have families alienated, loved ones sick and dying, people without jobs. To speak of Messiah's victory in these circumstances may sound like more wishful thinking, brave words, cold comfort, whistling in the dark.

In Romans 8, from which the text of the aria derives, Paul faces this paradox head-on. As the writer of Genesis imbues the story of creation with the tragedy of human existence, as the writer of Revelation projects the picture of human turmoil onto a vast cosmic screen, the apostle here reads the tribulations, the conflicts, the frustrations, the unresolved questions of our lives into the workings of the universe.

After the week of creation, "God saw everything that he had made, and indeed, it was very good" (Genesis 1:31). But things soon began to go amiss. After Adam's primal sin (and *adam* is the Hebrew word for "humanity") the orders of existence began to change. The woman had been taken from the side of the man, not from his head to rule him or from his feet to be ruled by him, but from his side as his partner. But now, as God speaks to Eve, he says that she will have pain in childbirth. She will still desire the man, but he will be her ruler (Genesis 3:16). The ground of her being has turned against her. The man was fashioned from the dust of the earth. The first thing God did with the man was to put him in the Garden and tell him to work it. Work was part of the conditions of paradise. But now he speaks to Adam, "Cursed is the ground because of you. . . . By the sweat of your face you shall eat bread until you return to the ground" (Genesis 3:17-19). The ground of his being has turned against him.

The fall left humanity at enmity with itself and left creation at enmity with humanity. The created universe shares in the devastation wrought by human sin. The keeper of the Garden has become the plunderer of the earth. And so, Paul writes, "The creation waits with eager longing for the revealing of the children of God" (Romans 8:19). The intent of God for the world was frustrated by human disobedience, so that all the created order yearns for salvation and renewal, "for the creation was subjected to futility, not of its own will but by the will of the one who subjected it [God, as part of Adam's punishment], in hope that the creation itself will be set free from its bondage to decay and will obtain the freedom of the glory of the children of God" (Romans 8:20-21). It looks forward to the new heaven and new earth to come about after Messiah's victory (Revelation 21:1). But in our days the creation struggles like a woman giving birth: "We know that the whole creation has been groaning in labor pains until now, and not only the creation, but we ourselves,

143

who have the first fruits of the Spirit, groan inwardly while we wait for adoption, the redemption of our bodies" (Romans 8:22-23).

And so "we hope for what we do not see, we wait for it with patience" (Romans 8:25), knowing that "all things work together for good for those who love God . . ." (Romans 8:28). This is so because God wills redemption; God knows our destiny.

So what does this amount to? Paul asks — and here we come to our text — "If God is for us, who is against us?" (Romans 8:31). Against God's determined will for our redemption, no threat, no danger, no affliction or grief can be effective. After all, he gave his Son for us. If he would do that, what good would he ultimately withhold? (Romans 8:32). Who can be so presumptuous as to fault those whom God has called? "Who will bring any charge against God's elect?" (Romans 8:33).

There are two ways to read what follows at this point. Since the Greek manuscripts contain no punctuation, it is at times difficult to know whether a sentence should be a question or a statement. The King James Version and the New Revised Standard Version give two questions, with a statement as a reply to each:

Q: Who will bring any charge against God's elect?
A: It is God who justifies.
Q: Who is to condemn?
A: It is Christ Jesus, who died, yes, who was raised. . . .

But the answers can be read as rhetorical questions, with obvious answers:

Q: Who will bring any charge against God's elect?
A: Is it God, the one who sets us right with himself? (No!)
Q: Who is to condemn?
A: Is it Christ Jesus, the one who was raised, who is at the right hand of God, who indeed intercedes for us? (No!)

The point is the same, either way one wishes to go, but the latter understanding sets us up for another question yet to come:

144

Q: Who will separate us from the love of Christ?
A: Will hardship, or distress, or persecution, or famine, or nakedness, or peril, or sword?" (Romans 8:35) — NO!

Hear now Paul's conclusion to the matter, and see how this passage will lead us in to the great apocalyptic chorus of praise that will end the oratorio.

No, in all these things we are more than conquerors through him who loved us. For I am convinced that neither death, nor life, nor angels, nor rulers, nor things present, nor things to come, nor powers, nor height, nor depth, nor anything else in all creation, will be able to separate us from the love of God in Christ Jesus our Lord. (Romans 8:37-39)

The final word of broken humanity has now been spoken, and it is a word that tears aside all created powers to express confidence that God's love for us is such, his fidelity to his covenant is such, that we are his forever. The last word from a mortal in the oratorio has now been uttered. The curtain separating time and eternity is about to be rent asunder, and the next words we hear will be those of our resurrected selves, singing praise to the Lamb of God.

## 53. CHORUS

Worthy is the Lamb that was slain, and hath redeemed us to God by His blood, to receive power, and riches, and wisdom, and strength, and honour, and glory, and blessing. *(Revelation 5:12b with interpolation from 5:9, modified)*

Blessing and honour, glory and pow'r be unto Him that sitteth upon the throne, and unto the Lamb, for ever and ever. Amen. *(Revelation 5:13b, 14a)*

Amen.

It is the end. A door in heaven opens, and we are ushered into the throne room of God. God is seated on the throne, but he is not described; all we are told is that his appearance is like jewels. Surrounding his throne are twenty-four thrones, on which are seated twenty-four elders, robed in white, with gold crowns.

In the biblical mind, the number three represented divine perfection: heaven, earth, and underworld; Father, Son, and Holy Spirit. Four stood for earthly completeness: Four directions, north, east, south, and west. Either the sum or the product of these numbers came to represent perfection: seven or twelve, which accounts for the frequent use of these numbers and their multiples in the Bible. Twenty-four, a number not elsewhere found in apocalyptic, is twice twelve, and the elders stand for the completeness of the church, incorporating the twelve tribes of Israel and the twelve disciples. They may have reminded the contemporary reader of the twelve men carrying fasces, symbols of imperial power, who stood about the Emperor Domitian in Rome (Revelation was possibly written during Domitian's reign in the late nineties of the first century).

Before God's throne is a sea of glass. Two factors operate here. First, glass was a rare and costly material in the ancient world. Second, this sea is still. The Hebrews were never seafarers; the coastline of Palestine is smooth, with no natural harbors. They were not at home on the sea; it was a realm of death and terror. Here it is stilled and unthreatening. When the new earth comes into being in Revelation 21:1, there will be no seas.

At the sides of the throne are four living creatures representing all of the created order: a lion — wild animals and nobility; an ox — domestic animals and strength; a human being — wisdom; an eagle — swiftness. All creation constantly intones: "Holy, Holy, Holy!"

We behold the one on the throne displaying a scroll, a scroll sealed with seven seals. A person's last will and testament would ordinarily have been sealed with seven seals, each seal being the impress of the person's own signet ring. The scroll is the will of God, sealed and guaranteed by his own imprint. But no one can be found in heaven, on earth, or in the underworld who is worthy to open the scrolls. We grieve at this, but we are assured by one of the elders: "Do not weep. See, the Lion of the tribe of Judah, the Root of David, has conquered, so that he can open the scroll and its seven seals" (Revelation 5:5). The reference is to the Messiah, a symbol going back to the messianic interpretation of Jacob's blessing on Judah in Genesis 49:8-12. But when we look to see this Lion, we see instead a Lamb — the Lamb of God — a Lamb having all power and all wisdom (seven horns and seven eyes). The Lamb has been slaughtered, but yet he stands and receives the scroll, as well as the adulation of the living creatures and the elders.

Then there is a sound. Many angels appear around the scene of the throne and the lamb and the living creatures and the elders — tens and tens and tens of thousands of angels (a "myriad" is a Greek term for ten thousand). The angels sing with full voice:

"Worthy is the Lamb that was slaughtered to receive power and wealth and wisdom and might and honor and glory and blessing!" (Revelation 5:12)

The words of the blessing are a feeble attempt of the created order to praise the Messiah. What will he do with wealth? Does not he already possess wisdom and might? How can he be said to receive it from his worshipers? He cannot, of course. All things are his. We can only borrow thoughts from own experience: wealth that contrasts with poverty, might that contrasts with feebleness; glory that contrasts with disgrace and squalor. Our lives are lived out on a plane between such opposite extremes. But in this scene the continuum vanishes. All has become glory, honor, majesty, and it is all that of God and the Lamb.

When this song has been sung, all creation is summoned forth to join in praise: "Then I heard every creature in heaven and on earth and under the earth and in the sea, and all that is in them, singing,

"To the one seated on the throne and to the Lamb be blessing and honor and glory and might forever and ever!" (Revelation 5:13)

"And the four living creatures said, 'Amen.'" *Amen* is a Hebrew word meaning "indeed, truly." It does not mean "the end." When someone in the congregation agrees with what the preacher says and shouts "Amen," she is using the real meaning of the word. We use it at the end of prayer to signify our affirmation of what has been said. In a unique usage, Jesus used it to introduce some of his sayings, those beginning in translation, "Truly, truly I tell you."

"And the elders fell down and worshiped." (Revelation 5:14)

~

THIS CHORUS, not Hallelujah, is the proper ending for *Messiah*. A stately chord in the bass sounds, and then over it are raised the worshiping voices. The words of the blessing are deliberately pronounced by all four vocal lines together. The frequent rests produce a staccato effect suggesting the constant bowing down of the creatures and elders before the throne.

The blessing is repeated, before the tenor and bass enter more energetically with the song of creation: "Blessing and honor, glory and power. . . ." The line is taken up by the sopranos, and soon the entire choir is tossing the lines about, playing with them in ecstatic praise. The marshaled energy of the chorus begins to focus on the phrase "forever and ever," in repeated descending lines that finally converge for the last *adagio,* "forever and ever," ending on the dominant chord of D major.

That dominant chord is resolved into the tonic D major by the massive Amen that ends the work. Audiences must be patient. This Amen, this affirmation of Messiah's coming, victory, and reign, must be savored, from the opening fugue, which like the sounding trumpet summons forth the living and the dead ("The Trumpet Shall Sound" is also in D major), to the final chords.

"Amen. Come, Lord Jesus!" (Revelation 22:20).